vocabmonster ™

250 SAT WORDS

The easy way to memorize and retain
hundreds of SAT words...in no time flat!

Created by specialists with
over a half-century of experience

www.vocabmonster.com

About Us

The Seasoned Team

VocabMonster boasts an expert team – a vocabulary expert, seasoned cartoonist, skilled technical specialists, and first-rate supporting team – with more than a half-century of experience. Through their efforts and commitment, VocabMonster is poised to take its place as the optimal learning resource in building a masterful vocabulary.

Rays of Sun, Inc.

VocabMonster's parent company, Rays of Sun, Inc., came up with the concept of an integrated website, books, ebooks, SmartPhone and tablet apps, using the proven science of mnemonics. The technical team boasts more than 25 years of experience.

David Freeling, Writer and Vocabulary Expert

David Freeling has been helping students ace the SAT and a wide range of other important exams since 1997. As founder and director of San Francisco-based Insight Tutoring, he has helped hundreds of students improve their fundamental English and math skills. In addition to writing *VocabMonster*, he is the co-author of *Barron's 6 GRE Practice Tests* and *Barron's GRE Math Workbook*. David offers a free library of videos focused on test-prep strategies online at www.NoeValleyTutor.com.

Ron Coleman, Cartoonist

Ron Coleman has been cartooning for over 50 years and concurrently held supportive positions at Paramount Pictures, 20th Century Fox, Orion Pictures, and Walt Disney studios. His primary website is www.colemantoons.com.

Kimberly Martin, Publisher

Kimberly Martin offers over 10 years of experience in working with small publishing companies and self-publishing authors to help them get their books formatted and published. She also provides individual coaching and workshops to educate authors on all aspects of the self-publishing process.

Jill Shtulman, Marketing Communication Specialist

Jill Shtulman is a seasoned strategic and creative professional with over 25 years of solid experience. She has worked steadily with Fortune 500 organizations as well as emerging and mid-sized companies, taking them to their next level of growth. Her website is www.jsacreative.com.

Contents

Introduction

Welcome to a better, more effective way to master vocabulary skills.

There's no doubt: a strong vocabulary is crucial to increasing SAT scores. Yet, who among us wants to spend hours of time learning words through dry, all-text presentations and rote memorization?

Fortunately, there's a much more efficient – and fun – way to learn vocabulary words. VocabMonster is based on the proven science of mnemonics: an effective technique that makes it easy for you to remember a word by associating it with a clever cartoon, mixed with humor and visual cues. It works!

It's an excellent way to memorize hundreds of words that appear most frequently on the SAT exams...and to keep them memorized *forever. No resource offers you MORE!*

Haughty

arrogant, disdainful, proud, snobbish

Think of: **Height of T**

A simple, clear definition is presented for each word, and important synonyms for the word are given in boldface, when applicable.

By thinking of humorous word associations that sound like the real word, you are far more likely to easily recall the word and retain the meaning.

Our cartoons are illustrated by a leading specialist with over 50 years of experience. Each one is designed to make vocabulary learning FUN and effective.

THE HEIGHT OF T GAVE THE IMPRESSION THAT HE WAS HAUGHTY AND LOOKED DOWN ON THE OTHERS.

- The **haughty** princess rarely condescends to speak to mere commoners.

Each word is placed in a sentence, so you can clearly understand how to use the word in 'real life'

Accolade

any award, honor, or expression of approval or praise

Think of: **A college aide**

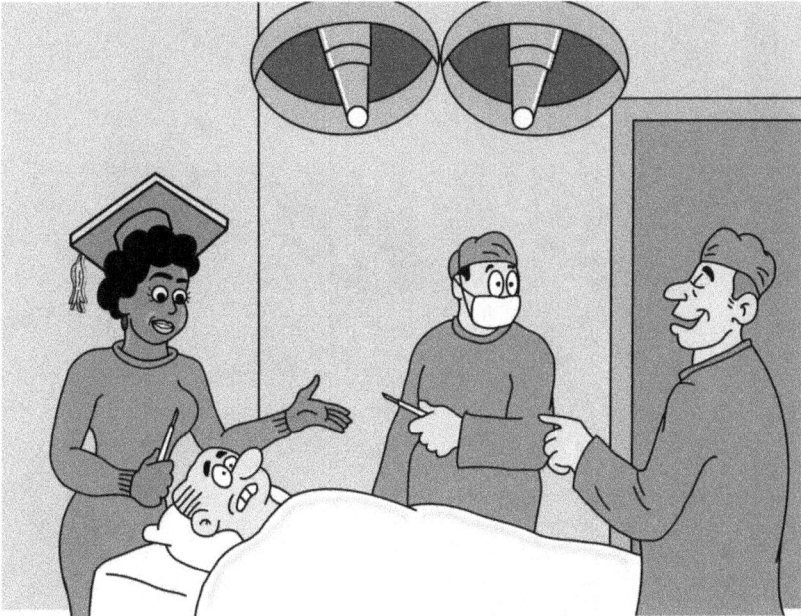

" SHE MAY BE JUST <u>A COLLEGE AIDE</u>, BUT SHE DESERVES GREAT ACCOLADES FOR HER KNOWLEDGE OF NEUROLOGICAL PROCEDURES. "

- *Slumdog Millionaire*, a charming film about surmounting poverty and class divides in India, won **accolades** at the Golden Globe Award Ceremonies. (Note: to ***surmount*** = to overcome)

- Arelyn Mahan, a Maryland principal, won **accolades** in her profession by demonstrating a true devotion to her students and teachers.

Clandestine

kept or done in secret; concealed

Think of: **Clan is destined**

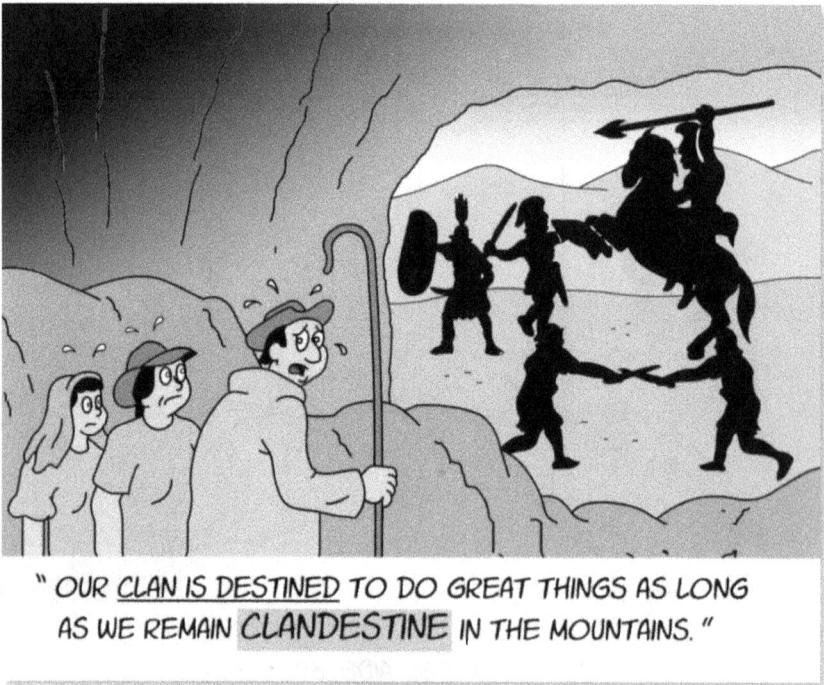

" OUR CLAN IS DESTINED TO DO GREAT THINGS AS LONG
AS WE REMAIN CLANDESTINE IN THE MOUNTAINS. "

- The police have been vigilant about searching for illegal, **clandestine** drug labs in this area.

- Few people know that a top United States commander in the Middle East ordered the expansion of **clandestine** military operations in the region in 2010.

Arcane

known or understood by very few; mysteriously obscure; **esoteric**

Think of: **R-cane**

SHHH ! DON'T TELL ANYONE ! R-CANES ARE BETTER !

R-Cane Factory
TOP SECRET

AN ELF FAVORS JOEY AND LEADS HIM TO THE ARCANE SOCIETY OF R-CANE ELVES.

- Dr. K's fascination with esoteric Byzantine history has led him to an **arcane** field of knowledge that is shared by only a handful of researchers on earth.

- In 2008, the website MightyQuiz began to allow users to quiz each other and attempt to stump strangers with their **arcane** knowledge.

Candid

honest, open, sincere, frank, outspoken

Think of: **Candied**

" LET ME BE CANDID WITH YOU, YOU NEED TO STOP
EATING SO MANY CANDIED APPLES. "

- TV show host Oprah Winfrey speaks **candidly** about her struggles to control her weight.

- After years of denial, the politician finally gave a **candid** confession of the crimes he had committed.

Mundane

common, ordinary, everyday, relating to matters of this world

Think of: **Monday**

AFTER A GREAT WEEKEND, GOING BACK TO SCHOOL ON MONDAY SEEMED RATHER MUNDANE.

- While some people have grandiose visions of improving the world or saving the planet, others have the more **mundane** dream of simply earning a decent living.

- On my backpacking jaunt through Eastern Europe, I discovered many fascinating regions and cultural differences, but some areas seemed rather **mundane**.

Emphatic

expressed with emphasis; forceful and insistent

Think of: **M, the Fatty**

IN DISCUSSING HIS VIEWS, <u>M, THE FATTY</u>, WAS ALWAYS VERY
EMPHATIC ABOUT WHAT HE BELIEVED.

- Louise gave an **emphatic** plea to the mayor to restore funding for the homeless.

- Despite the controversy surrounding string theory, physicist Michael Green **emphatically** supports it, believing that the elegant "theory of everything" will ultimately be proven.

Equitable

fair, just, reasonable

Think of: **Equal table**

" MOM, THIS IS SO UNFAIR. PLEASE BE EQUITABLE AND BUY ME AN EQUAL TABLE. "

- The basketball players and owners are seeking a solution that both sides will find fair and **equitable**.

- In the year 2011, 57 years after the landmark Brown vs. Board of Education Supreme Court decision, leaders in Huntsville, Alabama still had to demand access to **equitable** educational opportunities for black students.

Belligerent

inclined to fight; aggressive, hostile, warlike

Think of: **Belly**

A *BELLIGERENT* PERSON IS WILLING TO PUNCH SOMEONE RIGHT IN THE BELLY.

- The student became **belligerent** and aggressive when asked to leave the room and report to the principal.
- In 2011, U.S. Defense Secretary Robert Gates urged the dictatorship of North Korea to end its **belligerent** acts and cease aggressive actions against its neighbors.

Robust

strong and healthy, vigorous, hardy

Think of: **Robe bust**

FLEXING HIS ROBUST MUSCLES MADE HIS ROBE BUST.

- When Somali pirates took piracy to an almost industrial level, disrupting global trade, the world demanded a **robust** response.

- New intelligence software and technology have given our country some **robust** tools in the fight against terrorism.

Laconic

using few words; **terse**

Think of: **Lake on Nick**

WITH A LAKE ON NICK, HE ONLY HAD TIME FOR A LACONIC REMARK.

BUMMER !

- The senator's **laconic** answers frustrated reporters, who found his remarks to be curt, brief, and insubstantial.
- While Ed is quite sociable, his brother is extremely **laconic** and never says more than two words when we go to their house.

Review #1

1. He made an ____ appeal to Congress in defense of education and gave an impassioned plea to restore funding for the programs which had been cut.
   (A) Emphatic **(B)** Enigmatic **(C)** Illusory **(D)** Inadvertent **(E)** Ostentatious

2. We did not start this war; our neighbor's ____ acts of aggression, including the deployment of troops to the border, caused the conflict.
   (A) Innocuous **(B)** Belligerent **(C)** Gregarious **(D)** Affable **(E)** Discursive

3. His plans to start an underground, _____ movement dedicated to overthrowing the government were quickly discovered and thwarted.

   (A) Innocuous **(B)** Beneficial **(C)** Candid **(D)** Mundane **(E)** Clandestine

4. Ann's victory in the triathlon may be attributed to her ____ physical condition and intense training regimen.

   (A) Robust **(B)** Debilitated **(C)** Pathetic **(D)** Enervated **(E)** Laconic

5. The judge's decision may be considered _____ to all sides in the dispute and fair all around.

   (A) Candid **(B)** Belligerent **(C)** Robust **(D)** Clandestine **(E)** Equitable

6. His two-word, _____ response to a serious question frustrated the audience.
   (A) Laconic **(B)** Candid **(C)** Equitable **(D)** Verbose **(E)** Insightful

7. Arcane
   (A) Old or ancient **(B)** Obscure or esoteric **(C)** Wide open **(D)** Diligent **(E)** Tedious

8. Candid
   (A) Robust or healthy **(B)** Corpulent or fat **(C)** Honest or open **(D)** Old-fashioned **(E)** Deceitful

9. Accolade
   (A) Trial **(B)** Disgrace or demerit **(C)** Hardships or adversity **(D)** Honor or award **(E)** Beginning or conception

10. Mundane
    (A) Meticulous and tidy **(B)** Open or honest **(C)** Known only to a few **(D)** Forceful and insistent **(E)** Common or ordinary

Indomitable

Difficult to subdue, incapable of being defeated or conquered

Think of: **Not dominate-able**

THIS BULL POSSESSES AN INDOMITABLE SPIRIT AND IS NOT DOMINATE-ABLE, REFUSING TO SUBMIT TO THE PUNY MATADORS.

- The athlete's personal courage and **indomitable** self-confidence enabled him to return from a devastating injury and lead his team to a championship.

- The film *The **Indomitable** Teddy Roosevelt* is an inspiring documentary depicting the President's stubborn, headstrong determination.

Pedestrian

1. common, ordinary, dull, undistinguished 2. a person who walks

Think of: **Pedestrian**

COMPARED TO SKATEBOARDING, UNICYCLING AND POGO STICKING, BEING A PEDESTRIAN IS THE PEDESTRIAN WAY TO GET AROUND.

- While New York University students generally have a high regard for former President Bill Clinton, many found his commencement speech to be rather **pedestrian**.

- The governor's **pedestrian** response to a complex problem made people think that she relied on stock solutions and could not find innovative answers.

Placate

to **appease**, **pacify**, **mollify**, calm, or make someone less angry and upset

Think of: **Place to skate**

THE RINK MANAGER TRIED TO PLACATE THE ANGRY PLAYERS BY OFFERING THEM A NEW PLACE TO SKATE.

- The Roman poet Juvenal coined the phrase "bread and circuses" to refer to the way politicians could **placate** the angry masses by offering them cheap food and entertainment.

- The city of San Antonio built the 65,000 seat stadium known as the Alamodome largely to **placate** the demands of the San Antonio Spurs for a larger basketball venue.

Circumscribe

1. to limit narrowly or restrict, 2. to draw a circle around

Think of: **Circle inside**

BECAUSE THE ANGRY PIT BULL WAS TETHERED ON A SHORT
LEASH, ITS MOVEMENT WAS SEVERELY CIRCUMSCRIBED,
AND IT WAS CONFINED <u>INSIDE</u> A SMALL CIRCLE.

- The strict code of regulations within the housing community severely **circumscribes** the choice of colors that home owners can use to paint their houses.

- The geometry student was asked to use a compass to **circumscribe** the regular hexagon.

Bolster

1. *verb* – to support, prop up, uphold, buoy, or hearten
2. *noun* – a support

Think of: **Boost**

"THE HOT CHOCOLATE **BOLSTERED** OUR SAGGING SPIRITS -- GAVE US A BOOST."

- Jade **bolstered** her argument in support of food subsidies for the poor with several studies indicating the efficacy of such programs. (Note: *efficacy* = effectiveness)

- When performing floor exercises that involve leg lifts, many people use a small **bolster** under their lower back for support.

Embellish

to decorate, **adorn**, or make beautiful by adding ornamentation

Think of: **Bells**

ALTHOUGH MOST WEDDING CAKES ARE DECORATED WITH FLOWERS, THE CHEF DECIDED TO **EMBELLISH** THIS ONE WITH <u>BELLS</u>.

- Victorian-era homes in San Francisco were **embellished** with intricate architectural details and at least three bright colors of paint.
- Ann sought to **embellish** her appearance with ruby-red lipstick and a manicure.

Superficial

on the surface, not deep, shallow, concerned with only the obvious

Think of: **Super fishing**

- To judge people by their clothes and jewelry alone seems rather **superficial**.

- The report citing the risks of global warming was a useful but rather **superficial** warning because it skimmed the surface of the dangers but did not go into depth.

Dubious

doubtful, questionable, **skeptical**, of uncertain quality

Think of: **Doubt**

- The candidate's **dubious** background as a drug dealer and gang member will be hard to overcome in the election.

- The student said that she studied all her vocabulary, but because she couldn't remember a single definition, I was **dubious** of her claim.

Erratic

lacking consistency or regularity, unpredictable, wandering off-course

Think of: **Ear Attic**

- Joe's test scores in math this year have been **erratic**, with a failing grade often following an A+.

- When driving a car, stay clear of **erratic** drivers, who swerve inconsistently between lanes.

Judicious

having or showing good judgment, wise, sensible, **prudent**

Think of: **Judge**

THE <u>JUDGE</u> KEEPS ORDER IN THE COURT BY THE JUDICIOUS USE OF HIS GAVEL.

- Even many pacifists would agree that a **judicious** use of force is sometimes necessary in cases of self-defense or opposition to a clear moral wrong.

- Although Malik wanted to travel the world after graduation, he made the **judicious** decision to first get a job, in order to save money for the trip.

1. The student tried to _____ his argument with many examples and supporting documents.

    (A) Bolster **(B)** Placate **(C)** Circumscribe **(D)** Enervate **(E)** Deride

2. The champion boxer had been nicknamed "The _____ Force," because he has never been defeated.

    (A) Superficial **(B)** Dubious **(C)** Indomitable **(D)** Pedestrian **(E)** Erratic

3. His musical performance was _____, including some amazing high points but also some lamentably weak and discordant parts.

    (A) Consistent **(B)** Erratic **(C)** Candid **(D)** Surreptitious **(E)** Laconic

4. The child's movements were severely _____ by the school's strict rules.

    (A) Archaic **(B)** Bolstered **(C)** Gregarious **(D)** Circumscribed **(E)** Placated

5. The judge made a logical, fair, and _____ decision after carefully considering all arguments in the case.

    (A) Judicious **(B)** Erratic **(C)** Arcane **(D)** Archaic **(E)** Enigmatic

6. Pedestrian

    (A) Ordinary **(B)** Exciting **(C)** Sleepy **(D)** Rapid **(E)** Complex

7. Placate

    (A) Irritate **(B)** Nettle **(C)** Soothe or calm **(D)** Exacerbate **(E)** Elevate

8. Embellish

    (A) Depress **(B)** Appease **(C)** Mitigate **(D)** Confound **(E)** Adorn

9. Superficial

    (A) At the bottom **(B)** In the back **(C)** At the edges **(D)** On the surface **(E)** First and foremost

10. Dubious

    (A) Expensive **(B)** Exemplary **(C)** Strict **(D)** Honest **(E)** Doubtful

Catalyst

1. a substance that starts or speeds up a chemical reaction,
2. a person or thing that precipitates or causes a change

Think of: **Cattle fist**

ON THE CATTLE, HIS FIST IS A CATALYST, MOVING THEM
ALONG MORE QUICKLY.

- Acids are often used as **catalysts** to trigger chemical reactions.
- His ten-day Buddhist meditation retreat served as a **catalyst** for the personal transformation that made him a more compassionate and spiritual person.

Anomaly

a deviation from the common rule or norm, an unusual occurrence

Think of: **A non-Molly**

WITH 19 GIRLS NAMED MOLLY IN MS. MULLIGAN'S CLASS, GERTRUDE WAS AN ANOMALY - A NON-MOLLY.

- To encounter a flock of Dodo birds on a stroll through Central Park would be a true **anomaly** because they have been extinct since the late 17th century.

- An unusual feature appearing upon a baby at birth, such as a third nipple or a sixth finger, is referred to as a "congenital **anomaly**." (Note: *congenital* = at birth.)

Mitigate

to lessen in force or intensity, to make less severe or harsh, to moderate or **alleviate**

Think of: **Mitt in the gate**

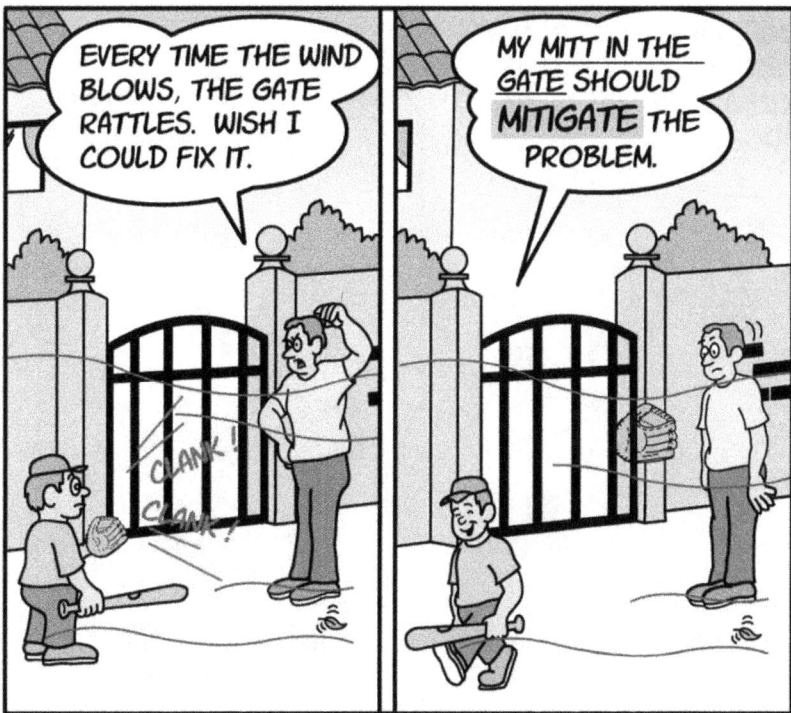

- The contractor hoped to **mitigate** the environmental impact of the new development by installing solar paneling on the roofs and by building around existing trees.

- The flood could not be avoided, but the townspeople hoped to **mitigate** its damage by piling thousands of heavy sandbags on the banks of the river.

Equivocate

to use vague, unclear, or ambiguous language, especially in order to avoid speaking directly and honestly

Think of: **Equal advocate**

I SUPPORT A CUT IN MILITARY SPENDING COUPLED WITH AN INCREASE IN THE MILITARY BUDGET.

GIVE PEACE A CHANCE

VOTE

DEFENSE CONTRACTS

SENATOR SPIEGEL **EQUIVOCATED** ON THE ISSUE OF MILITARY SPENDING BY ACTING AS AN EQUAL ADVOCATE TO BOTH SIDES OF THE CAUSE.

- Because the politician was willing to **equivocate** in her stance regarding the creation of green energy jobs, environmental advocates questioned her commitment to the cause.

- Because Carla **equivocated** to both Bob and Dan regarding who had won her true affections, the two boys felt confused and uncertain.

Hypothetical

assumed to exist; considered to exist only conditionally, as an idea or concept; supposed, conjectural

Think of: **Hippo the Tickle**

THE HIPPO ALWAYS DREAMED OF A *HYPOTHETICAL* WORLD, IN WHICH HE MASTERED HIS PREDATORS AS HIPPO THE TICKLE KING.

- In a **hypothetical** world in which no person would seek to take advantage of the system, your plans for ending poverty might work.

- Suppose, **hypothetically**, that someone offered you one million dollars to spend one year in jail. Would you take the offer?

Capricious

tending to make sudden changes; characterized by sudden whim; impulsive, unpredictable, **whimsical**, **fickle**

Think of: **Cap precious**

CAP PRECIOUS

DARN! I FORGOT MY BASEBALL CAP!

YOU CAN BORROW MINE.

THANKS. NO, YOU CAN'T!

? I GUESS YOU CAN...

NO ... YOU CAN'T!

THE <u>CAP</u> WAS SO <u>PRECIOUS</u> TO ISABELLE THAT SHE WAS CAPRICIOUS ABOUT LENDING IT AND KEPT CHANGING HER MIND.

- The mayor of the town argued that concerns about the new casino were not **capricious** whims targeted at any new development, but genuine worries about the crime that such an enterprise might bring to the area.

- In an aristocracy, or government by a small, privileged class, the **capricious** desires of a few powerful people can have harsh consequences for the masses.

Succinct

characterized by clear, precise expression in few words; uttered or written with brevity and clarity; **concise**, **terse**

Think of: **Sucks ink**

" IT'S A NEW HIGH-TECH ERASER. IF YOU WRITE TOO MUCH IT <u>SUCKS</u> AWAY THE EXTRA <u>INK</u>, LEAVING A CONCISE, SUCCINCT ESSAY. "

- Jason wrote a **succinct** summary of the book.

- Abraham Lincoln's Gettysburg Address, lasting less than two minutes but remembered through the ages, was the epitome of a **succinct** but forceful speech. (Note: *epitome* = prime example)

Curtail

to cut short, reduce, limit, **abridge**, or terminate

Think of: **Cut tail**

SADLY, THE VETERINARIAN HAD TO <u>CUT</u> THE SPIDER MONKEY'S INFECTED <u>TAIL</u>, SEVERELY *CURTAILING* ITS MOVEMENT.

- Cigarette smoking or illegal drug use by pregnant women can **curtail** the development of the fetus and result in congenital abnormalities.

- The military checkpoints placed at every major intersection were of dubious legality and effectively **curtailed** the flow of traffic throughout the city.

Conflagration

a large destructive fire

Think of: **Flags rationed**

FIRE SALE !

ONE FLAG PER CUSTOMER

FLAG FACTORY

AFTER THE CONFLAGRATION AT THE FLAG MANUFACTURING FACTORY, FLAGS WERE RATIONED.

- The firefighters were able to contain the **conflagration** only after ten long hours fighting the massive blaze.

- The introduction of the controversial new bill in Congress caused a **conflagration** of angry words and a firestorm of heated debate.

Prolific

producing abundantly and in large quantities, fertile, productive

Think of: **Pro lifter**

BUTCH IS A PROLIFIC WEIGHT-LIFTER: AS A PRO LIFTER, HE'S LIFTED MORE THAN EIGHT MILLION POUNDS DURING HIS CAREER.

- Author Joyce Carol Oates, who has written over 100 books in a 45-year career, is a very **prolific** writer of quality fiction and nonfiction.

- With nearly 50 original albums to his credit, Bob Dylan is considered one of the most **prolific** musicians of all time.

Review #3

1. The _____ author writes a new book every 4 months.
   (A) Tedious **(B)** Prolific **(C)** Pretentious **(D)** Malignant **(E)** Disingenuous

2. We had to keep changing the layout and design of the report to fit our boss's _____ whims.
   (A) Capricious **(B)** Unwavering **(C)** Candid **(D)** Succinct **(E)** Prolific

3. By choosing to _____ on the issue of reduced military spending, the senator tried to appeal to his allies and opponents alike, but only confused both sides.
   (A) Mitigate **(B)** Deprecate **(C)** Curtail **(D)** Equivocate **(E)** Inundate

4. For all the horrors of World War II, many people believe that in the U.S. the war at least served as a/an _____ triggering economic growth and finally lifting the country out of the Depression.
   (A) Conflagration **(B)** Accolade **(C)** Pedestrian **(D)** Catalyst **(E)** Deception

5. The _____ caused $4 million in fire damages.
   (A) Conflagration **(B)** Disintegration **(C)** Pedestrian **(D)** Anomaly
   (E) Aberration

6. Anomaly
   (A) Big fire **(B)** Flood **(C)** Unusual occurrence **(D)** Tedious response
   (E) Disheveled appearance

7. Mitigate
   (A) Worsen **(B)** Alleviate **(C)** Mystify **(D)** Deceive **(E)** Destroy

8. Hypothetical
   (A) Assumed to exist **(B)** Pretending to be skilled **(C)** Willfully contrived
   (D) Perceived as grandiose **(E)** Subject to mood changes

9. Succinct
   (A) Verbose **(B)** Productive **(C)** Out of place **(D)** Conjectural **(E)** Concise

10. Curtail
    (A) Elevate or lift **(B)** Reduce or end **(C)** Lessen the damage
    (D) Waver with uncertainty **(E)** Produce copiously

Epitome

a perfect representative of a class or type, a prime example, a person or thing that typifies the features of a whole class

Think of: **A Pit Tummy**

ZOE HAS A PIT-SIZE TUMMY AND IS THE EPITOME OF PHYSICAL FITNESS.

- Many people consider John D. Rockefeller to be the **epitome** of "the American Dream," because he grew up in a poor family but went on to found Standard Oil and become the world's first billionaire.

- Lucy's paper is the **epitome** of a well-written report because it is thoroughly researched and clearly explained.

Innocuous

harmless, not hurtful, unlikely to offend

Think of: **I knock you and us**

- His comment was intended to be **innocuous**, but his contemptuous, angry tone caused her to be offended.
- The hairline fracture in the bridge looked **innocuous**, but when the crack developed into a wider rift, thousands of drivers' lives were imperiled. (Note: *imperiled* = endangered)

Gregarious

sociable, friendly, fond of the company of others

Think of: **Greg is good in groups**

GREGARIOUS GREG IS GOOD IN GROUPS.

- Comedian Robin Williams is considered one of the more easygoing, **gregarious** celebrities.
- Jania's **gregarious** personality has earned her many friends.

Benevolent

kind, caring, compassionate, generous, **magnanimous**, **altruistic**, **philanthropic**

Think of: **Ben loves Every Needy Thing**

BECAUSE BEN LOVES EVERY NEEDY THING, HE IS ALWAYS DOING KIND DEEDS AND ACTING IN A BENEVOLENT WAY.

- Many religions require their followers to commit **benevolent** acts to benefit the poor and needy.

- Because Amelia always strives to help her fellow human beings, she is esteemed as a **benevolent** person. (Note: *esteemed* = highly regarded.)

Ephemeral

short-lived, **transient**, **transitory**, not lasting long, temporary, **fleeting**, impermanent

Think of: **F-emerald**

- The art of sand sculpting is **ephemeral**, because the intricate sculptures last only until high tide or the next wind storm.

- Josephine's reign as class president was, unfortunately, **ephemeral**, because a vote recount ended her term after two hours.

Transient

not lasting long, **ephemeral**, **fleeting**, short-lived, **transitory**

Think of: **In Transit**

" MOVE ALONG, ANN ! PLEASE <u>TRANSIT</u> OFF THE DIVING
BOARD. YOUR TIME UP THERE IS MEANT TO BE **TRANSIENT.** "

- Looking skyward, I saw for but a moment the image of a dragon in the **transient** clouds.

- Many people yearn for fame, but fame can be extremely **transient**, perhaps lasting only 15 minutes, or until the next hot story.

Dearth

lack, shortage, **scarcity**, an inadequate amount

Think of: **Earth**

- The army's **dearth** of weapons, food, and supplies led to its quick defeat.
- A **dearth** of teachers and resources at the nation's nursing schools has caused thousands of qualified applicants to be turned away.

Dilatory

intended to delay or postpone, causing a delay or waste of time

Think of: **Delay**

- All the rain has had a **dilatory** effect on the new construction project.

- The defendant's actions were **dilatory**; he had no chance of winning the case, so he could only resort to postponing the inevitable.

Enigma

mystery, riddle, puzzle, **conundrum**, something not easily explained

Think of: **E̲nergy I̲gloo M̲a**

- The role of black holes in the fabric of the universe is an **enigma** that has captured the interest of many physicists and astronomers.

- The expression on the face of *Mona Lisa* in Leonardo da Vinci's famous painting is considered **enigmatic** and open to many interpretations.

Corroborate

to give evidence of the truth of something, to confirm or make more certain

Think of: **Cory the robber ate**

- You claim you were at home when the crime was committed, but can anyone **corroborate** your claim?
- I have a witness who can **corroborate** my account of the car collision.

1. I have five witnesses who can _____ my account of the accident.
   (A) Deny **(B)** Mitigate **(C)** Equivocate **(D)** Curtail **(E)** Corroborate

2. Her behavior in class represents the _____ of good manners and proper composure.
   (A) Epitome **(B)** Anomaly **(C)** Dearth **(D)** Enigma **(E)** Conflagration

3. We'd better go play outside now and enjoy the beautiful day while it lasts, because the nice weather can be truly _____ in this city by the bay.
   (A) Enigmatic **(B)** Ephemeral **(C)** Innocuous **(D)** Belligerent **(E)** Gregarious

4. Your _____ tactics will only set us back briefly; you cannot permanently delay the inevitable.
   (A) Gregarious **(B)** Dilatory **(C)** Hypothetical **(D)** Succinct **(E)** Prolific

5. Although scientists have long known how to compute the force of gravity, how gravity actually works is still considered to be a/an _____ . It is only partially understood.
   (A) Abatement **(B)** Conflagration **(C)** Enigma **(D)** Epitome **(E)** Dearth

6. Innocuous
   (A) Hostile **(B)** Harmful **(C)** Sociable **(D)** Harmless **(E)** Inadvertent

7. Gregarious
   (A) Doing good **(B)** Short-lived **(C)** Lacking **(D)** Harmless **(E)** Sociable

8. Benevolent
   (A) Malevolent **(B)** Philanthropic **(C)** Aggressive, warlike **(D)** Warped **(E)** Causing delay

9. Transient
   (A) Temporary, short-lived **(B)** Rapid **(C)** Whimsical **(D)** Not causing harm **(E)** Charitable

10. Dearth
    (A) Abundance **(B)** Excess **(C)** Shortage **(D)** Mystery **(E)** Prime example

Opulent

wealthy, rich, **affluent**, abundantly supplied, characterized by an obvious or lavish display of wealth

Think of: **A pool lent**

AS PART OF HER *OPULENT* ESTATE, THE CELEBRITY OWNS AN EXTRA <u>POOL</u> WHICH IS <u>LENT</u> TO THE KIDS FROM TOWN WHEN THE WEATHER GETS HOT.

- Because the celebrity wore a $10,000 dress and multiple diamond necklaces, her appearance was an **opulent** display of her wealth.

- We were treated to a lavish feast in an **opulent** mansion belonging to one of the world's richest men. (Note: lavish = in great amounts, characterized by extravagance and **profusion**)

Articulate

1. adjective – expressing oneself in clear, effective language; well-spoken, **eloquent** 2. verb – to express in words clearly and coherently, to utter distinctly

Think of: **Article you ate**

- Mariah is an **articulate** public speaker.

- Many people attribute the success of Barack Obama in the 2008 election to his ability to forcefully **articulate** a vision for a better America.

Disheveled

unkempt, untidy, disarranged, in loose disarray or disorder

Think of: **This shovel**

- After surviving in the wilderness for 12 days, the fugitive had a **disheveled** appearance and a rancorous stench. (Note: *rancorous stench* = nasty odor.)

- While businessman Bob prefers a tidy appearance, surfer-dude Sal opts for the **disheveled** look.

Serene

calm, peaceful, **tranquil**, unruffled, unaffected by disturbance

Think of: **Screen**

- We spent a serene day by the lake, reading, meditating, and gazing at the calm water.

- The bookstore owner observed, "There must be twenty books on the market about how to achieve a serene state of mind."

Inevitable

unavoidable, certain to happen, impossible to avoid or prevent

Think of: **In every table**

"IT IS INEVITABLE THAT IN THE CENTER OF EVERY TABLE WE SET THE CANDLES."

- When the election results poured in and our candidate was ahead by 12 percentage points with 99% of the vote already counted, we knew victory was **inevitable**.

- The **inevitable** end for any insect unfortunate enough to be caught in the Black Widow's web is a venomous bite, followed by enzymatic digestion.

Tenacious

holding fast, keeping a firm grip, maintaining a firm hold

Think of: **Tennis ace**

SELENA HAS A **TENACIOUS** DESIRE TO BE A <u>TENNIS ACE</u>.
WE SEE HER PRACTICING HER SERVE DEEP INTO THE NIGHT.

- When the Warriors basketball team hunkered down to play a **tenacious** defense – with each player staying in dogged, relentless contact with his opponent – it finally won a game.

- The climber's **tenacious** pursuit of the mountaintop finally culminated in his reaching the summit at sunset.

Tenable

capable of being held, maintained, or defended

Think of: **Ten able**

- When Libyan rebel forces began to receive international support and NATO military help in early 2011, many analysts knew that Colonel Gadaffi's autocratic hold on power would not be **tenable** for much longer.

- Some people consider themselves religiously and spiritually inclined, even though they find the idea of an anthropomorphic deity to be no longer **tenable**. (Notes: *anthropomorphic* = in the form of a human; *deity* = god.)

Disparity

difference, inequality, gap

Think of: **Dis da party?**

THERE WAS QUITE A DISPARITY BETWEEN THE APPEARANCE OF THE WEDDING GUESTS AND THAT OF THE TWO GATE-CRASHERS.

- There was a large **disparity** in talent between the professional acting troupe and our school's own improvisational comedy team.

- In 1954, the United States Supreme Court ruled that a system of separate but equal schools for different races created an inherent **disparity** in educational quality.

Erudite

learned, scholarly, characterized by great and extensive knowledge

Think of: **Err you don't** (Note: to err = to make a mistake.)

- Funny author Lisa Bloom has been called "one of the smartest and most **erudite** people in the American popular culture."
- The **erudite** professor was able to speak at length on many subjects in a wide range of academic fields.

Archaic

characteristic of a much earlier, more primitive period; antiquated, old, ancient

Think of: **Arch**

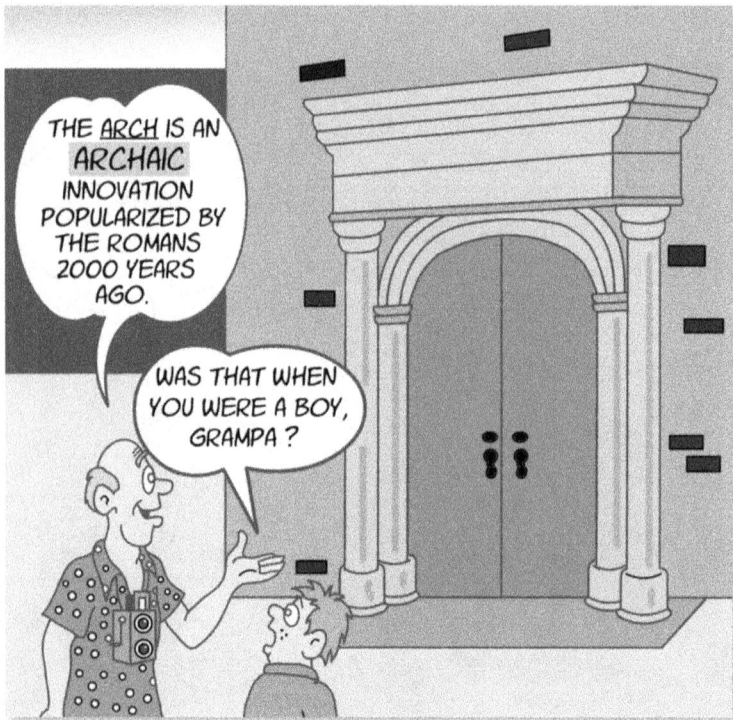

- While millions of Americans grew up on a pop culture defined by black and white televisions, rotary telephones, vinyl records, and turntables, today's youth view these gadgets as **archaic** technology.

- In watching the society of 19th century London depicted in the *Sherlock Holmes* dramas, I am struck by how **archaic** the horse-drawn carriage seems; though, at the time, these carriages must have been considered extremely modern.

1. Her gigantic mansion and garage full of antique cars were an _____ display of her wealth.

    (A) Archaic **(B)** Erudite **(C)** Inevitable **(D)** Opulent **(E)** Articulate

2. By playing a _____ defense and persistently sticking to our opponents, we were able to win the game.

    (A) Serene **(B)** Tenacious **(C)** Tenable **(D)** Disheveled **(E)** Dilatory

3. The stone tools and bone weapons on display at the museum typify an _____ era known as the Neolithic Age.

    (A) Archaic **(B)** Articulate **(C)** Inevitable **(D)** Opulent **(E)** Innocuous

4. The king's grasp on power was no longer _____ in the face of the peasant revolt.

    (A) Erudite **(B)** Articulate **(C)** Tenacious **(D)** Tenable **(E)** Archaic

5. Joe is an _____ speaker of Italian and French, and can express his ideas in at least 3 languages.

    (A) Enigmatic **(B)** Opulent **(C)** Articulate **(D)** Inevitable **(E)** Ephemeral

6. Disheveled

    (A) Neat **(B)** Certain to happen **(C)** Difference or gap **(D)** Peaceful
    (E) Sloppy, messy

7. Serene

    (A) Peaceful **(B)** Hostile **(C)** Sleepy **(D)** Learned **(E)** Ancient

8. Inevitable

    (A) Lacking **(B)** Calm and relaxed **(C)** Relentless or persistent
    (D) Maintainable **(E)** Certain to happen

9. Disparity

    (A) Lack or scarcity **(B)** Difference or gap **(C)** Prime example
    (D) Something that causes a change **(E)** Mystery or riddle

10. Erudite

    (A) Rude **(B)** Harmless **(C)** Learned **(D)** Messy **(E)** Peaceful

Appease

to bring a state of peace or calm; to soothe, calm, **pacify**, **placate**, or **mollify**

Think of: **Apple, please**

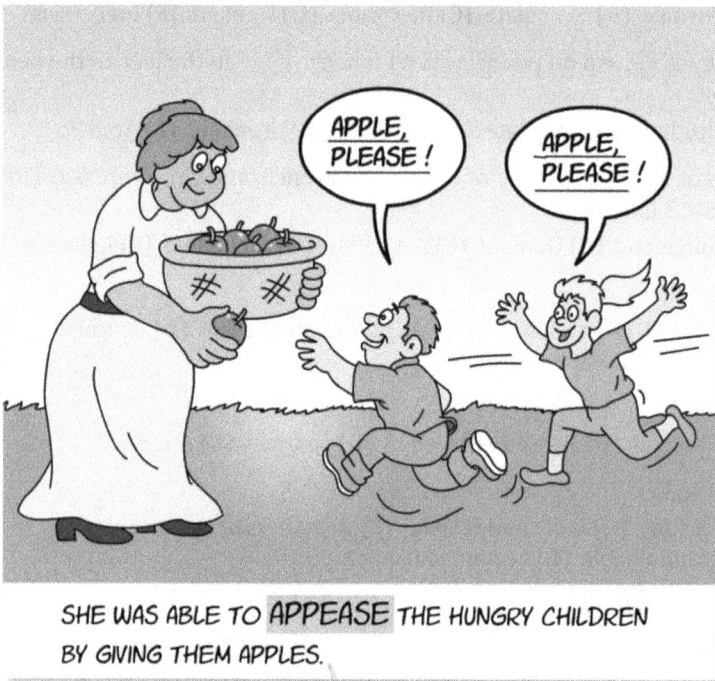

SHE WAS ABLE TO **APPEASE** THE HUNGRY CHILDREN BY GIVING THEM APPLES.

- When the Egyptian leader agreed to minor government reforms, the gesture was insufficient to **appease** the angry crowds in the streets, who demanded his ouster after nearly three decades in power. (Note: to **oust** = remove or expel.)

- On their hike up the enchanted volcano, the brave adventurers feared that only a human sacrifice would **appease** the angry volcano gods, whose sacred ground had been encroached upon.

Exorbitant

exceeding all bounds of custom or reason in amount or extent; highly excessive

Think of: **Out of orbit**

- The **exorbitant** rent that she pays prevents her from being able to afford luxuries, such as eating out and cable TV.

- The **exorbitant** prices at the chic new restaurant have dissuaded me from dining there.

Monotony

wearisome uniformity or lack of variety

Think of: **Mo not Tony**

I LIKE THE NAME TONY TO GO ALONG WITH THE TWINS, TIM AND TOM.

THOSE NAMES ARE TOO SIMILAR AND COMMON. LET'S GO WITH MO, NOT TONY.

SHE PICKS THE NAME MO, NOT TONY, TO BREAK THE MONOTONY.

- He enjoyed the salary of his new job, but not the **monotony**; his tasks were repetitive, and he did the same thing all day long.

- Ann found life in the religious monastery to be a boring **monotony** of repetitious lectures and the same prayers every day.

Surreptitious

obtained or done by stealth; unauthorized, secret, sneaky

Think of: **Sarah's pet vicious**

WHAT MAKES SARAH'S PET VICIOUS? IT SNEAKS UP BEHIND YOU. IT'S SURREPTITIOUS.

- Zoe's **surreptitious** mission in the game is to sneak into Ellen's house and secretly snap a picture of her family members while they're asleep.

- The term "phishing" refers to any **surreptitious** attempt to obtain a person's sensitive information online. Phishing includes various types of hoaxes and scams.

Futile

having no practical effect or useful result; ineffective

Think of: **Few tiles**

" IT'S *FUTILE* TO TRY TO FINISH THIS BATHROOM. THERE ARE TOO FEW TILES. "

- Once the evil revolutionary government took complete control of the country and began to rule with an iron fist, popular resistance to their regime became **futile**.

- The family made one last **futile** attempt to save the business before realizing that they would have to close their doors due to a lack of clients.

Onerous

burdensome, taxing, laborious, having obligations

Think of: **The owner is us**

- Stan's family had the **onerous** task of trying to clean and restore the house after the hurricane and flood hit.

- In Greek mythology, the legendary titan, Atlas, is forced to take on the **onerous** burden of carrying the weight of the world on his shoulders.

Autonomy

independence, self-reliance, self-government

Think of: **A ton of money**

NOW THAT SHE HAS INHERITED A TON OF MONEY, SHE HAS ACHIEVED SOME **AUTONOMY** FROM HER PARENTS.

- Many children look forward to the day that they will come of age, support themselves, and achieve **autonomy** from their parents.

- The U.S. wanted to ensure that the new, democratic government in Iraq achieved **autonomy** before withdrawing troops from the country.

Penchant

liking, taste, tendency or fondness for something;
proclivity, **predilection**, inclination, **predisposition**,
propensity

Think of: **Bench ant**

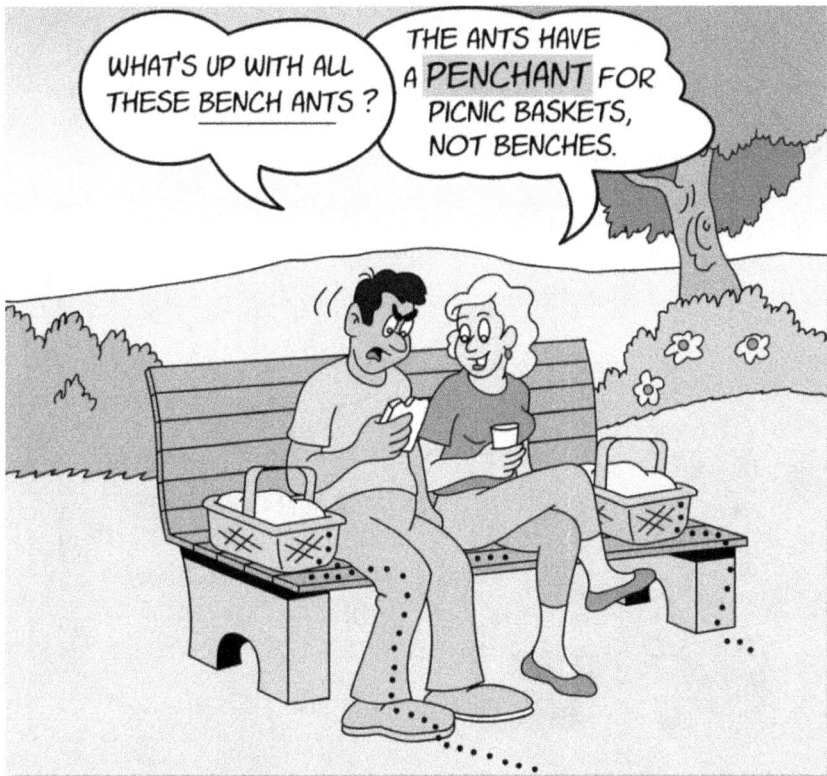

- Andres has a **penchant** for vanilla ice cream.
- Jeremy has a **penchant** for hiding his little sister's toys, much to her frustration and anger.

Disparage

to belittle, criticize, mock, **reproach**, **denigrate**, or speak of slightingly

Think of: **This Pa Raged**

- If you **disparage** my plans for growing this business, let's hear your ideas.
- The actor's contract prohibits him from **disparaging** the movie in public appearances.

Iconoclast

a person who attacks cherished traditions or beliefs, one who seeks to overthrow traditional ideas or institutions

Think of: **Icons won't last**

YOU'RE PUTTING YOUR PORTRAITS OF GANDHI, JESUS, JFK AND LINCOLN INTO STORAGE. HOW COME ?

I HAVE A NEW WAY OF DOING THINGS.

AN *ICONOCLAST* MAKES SURE THAT THE ICONS WON'T LAST.

- The **iconoclast** encouraged all followers of the church to question their beliefs and seek new core values.

- The filmmaker Robert Altman is considered an **iconoclast** because he took movies in unexplored directions and challenged the traditional limitations of Westerns and other genres of film.

1. We faced the _____ task of having to climb the mountain while carrying 50-pound backpacks.
   (A) Exorbitant **(B)** Monotonous **(C)** Surreptitious **(D)** Futile **(E)** Onerous

2. Joaquin found his fast food job of flipping meat all day to be rather _____.
   (A) Exorbitant **(B)** Monotonous **(C)** Surreptitious **(D)** Futile **(E)** Onerous

3. Because the prices at the new store were _____ and outrageously high, it attracted very few customers.
   (A) Exorbitant **(B)** Monotonous **(C)** Surreptitious **(D)** Futile **(E)** Onerous

4. Since our army is outnumbered ten-to-one and surrounded, resistance is _____ ; we had better surrender.
   (A) Exorbitant **(B)** Monotonous **(C)** Surreptitious **(D)** Futile **(E)** Onerous

5. His _____ attempt to sneak out of class by creating a distraction in the corner of the room with a whoopee cushion landed him in detention.
   (A) Exorbitant **(B)** Monotonous **(C)** Surreptitious **(D)** Futile **(E)** Onerous

6. Appease
   (A) Placate or pacify **(B)** Extremely expensive **(C)** Limit or restrict
   (D) Boost or support **(E)** Reduce or end

7. Autonomy
   (A) Inequality **(B)** Person who goes against tradition **(C)** Inclination
   (D) Independence **(E)** Big fire

8. Disparity
   (A) Preference or predisposition **(B)** Difference or gap **(C)** Self-reliance
   (D) A rebel or nonconformist **(E)** Shortage or scarcity

9. Iconoclast
   (A) Independence **(B)** Shortage or scarcity **(C)** Difference or gap
   (D) Preference or predisposition **(E)** Person who challenges traditional beliefs

10. Penchant
    (A) Shortage or scarcity **(B)** Difference or gap **(C)** Preference or predisposition
    (D) Person who challenges tradition **(E)** Independence

Disingenuous

not sincere, lacking candor and honesty

Think of: **Not genuine**

- The con man tried to convince the woman that his **disingenuous** tale was true.

- Tina believed the young man's gesture of friendship to be a **disingenuous** attempt to land a job at her father's company.

Effusive

demonstrative, gushing, giving extravagant expression of feelings

Think of: **A few sieves**

I REALLY LOVE YOUR AWESOME KITCHEN. IT'S AMAZING. GREAT UTENSILS. YOU EVEN HAVE A FEW EXCELLENT SIEVES.

RICK IS EFFUSIVE IN PRAISING HIS FRIEND'S KITCHEN, WHICH EVEN HAS A FEW SIEVES.

- The guests **effusively** thanked their hosts for the meal and free place to stay.

- President Obama garnered **effusive** praise – even from his detractors – when he ordered the successful mission against Osama bin Laden. (Note: to *garner* = to gather or earn.)

Taciturn

quiet, silent, not talkative, reserved

Think of: **Tass's turn**

- The **taciturn** child sat alone in the corner without saying a word.
- The **taciturn** 30th President of the United States, Calvin Coolidge, was famous for monosyllabic replies.

Tactile

relating to the sense of touch, capable of being perceived by touch, **tangible**

Think of: **Tack tile**

- Many blind people develop a heightened **tactile** sense and are able to read Braille with their fingers as well as sighted people read print.

- Sophie was blindfolded and led through a "**tactile** maze," which she had to feel her way out of.

Lament

to express grief, sorrow, or regret about something; to mourn

Think of: **Lame ant**

ALL THE INSECTS IN THE FOREST **LAMENT** THE FATE OF THE LAME ANT.

- I **lament** the disappearance of the rainforests.
- When Martin Luther King Jr. was assassinated, people all over the world **lamented** the loss of a great leader for social change.

Multifaceted

having many facets, aspects, or parts

Think of: **Multi-faced-Ted**

- Whereas Author A's characters all seem one-dimensional, Author B's characters are fully developed and **multifaceted**.

- Our plan to promote economic growth and reduce poverty must be **multifaceted** and tackle issues in all strata of society. (Notes: *strata* = levels or layers, ***stratified*** = layered by rank or ability.)

Deleterious

causing harm or injury; harmful or hurtful

Think of: **Delete Russ**

" DON'T DELETE RUSS FROM YOUR PLAY. HE'S THE FUNNIEST CHARACTER. DELETING RUSS WILL HAVE A DELETERIOUS EFFECT ON THE PLAY. "

- The **deleterious** effects of cigarette smoke on human health have been widely documented.

- Consumption of alcohol or drugs by a pregnant woman can have a **deleterious** impact on the developing baby.

Hackneyed

made commonplace and stale by overuse; **trite**, **cliché**

Think of: **Hack the knees**

DON'T HACK THE KNEES ! THAT'S SO HACKNEYED. THEY'LL CALL YOU ON IT EVERY TIME.

- The writer's ideas all seemed **hackneyed** – I believe I've read each of her sentences a dozen times in various publications.

- "Give peace a chance," is a rather **hackneyed** phrase that still conveys a nugget of wisdom.

Facetious

amusing, humorous, silly, not intended to be taken seriously

Think of: **Face tie us**

" THE NEW FACE-TIE LOOK SPORTED BY US IS MEANT TO BE FACETIOUS. "

- Harry wore his tie up on his face, in part to be **facetious** and in part to rebel against the very idea of having to wear a tie.

- After the crowded car nearly struck another vehicle on the freeway, John made a **facetious** remark about Maya's driving that amused some but offended others.

Espouse

to adopt, embrace, or support a cause; to take in marriage

Think of: **Spouse**

" YOU'RE MY <u>SPOUSE</u>. OF COURSE I WILL ESPOUSE YOUR PLANS BEFORE THE COMMITTEE. "

- The President **espoused** the new bill and claimed it would put millions of people back to work.

- I **espouse** the compromise measures that were proposed by the wise new principal.

1. The _____ child hardly said a word all day.
    (A) Effusive **(B)** Taciturn **(C)** Multifaceted **(D)** Facetious **(E)** Disingenuous

2. Consuming too much food and drink will have a _____ effect on your health.
    (A) Multifaceted **(B)** Taciturn **(C)** Deleterious **(D)** Tactile **(E)** Facetious

3. Tyreke was _____ in his praise of the generous feast: he repeatedly thanked and complimented his hosts.
    (A) Effusive **(B)** Disingenuous **(C)** Deleterious **(D)** Tactile **(E)** Facetious

4. I found her story to be _____; I knew she was lying and trying to mislead me.
    (A) Effusive **(B)** Deleterious **(C)** Facetious **(D)** Disingenuous **(E)** Hackneyed

5. The boys wrapped her whole house in toilet paper, a prank they intended as _____ and funny, but the girl found their actions to be immature and juvenile rather than amusing.
    (A) Tactile **(B)** Hackneyed **(C)** Facetious **(D)** Multifaceted **(E)** Effusive

6. The story's _____ language diminished the impact of its ideas, because the author resorted to using tired clichés rather than original wording.
    (A) Hackneyed **(B)** Multifaceted **(C)** Taciturn **(D)** Deleterious **(E)** Clandestine

7. Because the software application is so _____ and has so many different components and layers, only an expert could understand it.
    (A) Clandestine **(B)** Hackneyed **(C)** Disingenuous **(D)** Tactile **(E)** Multifaceted

8. Tactile
    (A) Quiet **(B)** Secret or hidden **(C)** Extremely expensive
    (D) Capable of being touched **(E)** Friendly

9. Lament
    (A) Mourn or regret **(B)** Anger or inflame **(C)** Speed up **(D)** Criticize or rebuke
    (E) Suppress or prevent

10. Espouse
    (A) Soothe of pacify **(B)** Speed up **(C)** Criticize or insult
    (D) Support or embrace **(E)** Destroy

Florid

excessively ornate, flowery, flushed with rosy color

Think of: **Flowered**

THE *FLORID* DESIGN OF THE FLOWERED CAKE WAS ABOUT TO GET MESSED UP BY SOME REAL FLOWERS.

- I was not convinced by the author's **florid** writing style; the ornate prose could not conceal major plot flaws and a lack of motivation for the characters' actions.

- Gasping for breath after her long jog, Gretchen appeared in our midst, her **florid** face glowing red in the white moonlight of a cold winter night.

Affable

warm and friendly, pleasant, easy-going

Think of: **Laughable**

BECAUSE ZOE FINDS MOST OF LIFE'S PROBLEMS LAUGHABLE, PEOPLE CONSIDER HER TO BE EASY-GOING AND AFFABLE.

- Devin is **affable** and makes friends with ease.
- Traci's **affable** demeanor during the catastrophe reassured the rest of us, who were all panicking.

Berate

to scold, rebuke, or criticize

Think of: **Bear ate**

- The teacher **berated** the student for trying to cheat.
- The parent **berated** his child for dumping the bucket of paint on the floor.

Expedite

to speed up or hasten; to accomplish promptly, quickly, and efficiently

Think of: **X sped**

X SPED ALL THE WAY TO THE FINISH LINE, **EXPEDITING** HIS VICTORY !

- Turning off the television while studying will **expedite** the learning process.

- Because the refugees needed to flee the country quickly, they hoped the border officials would **expedite** their passport applications.

Morose

having a withdrawn, gloomy personality; moody, sour, **surly, melancholy**

Think of: **Mo rose**

GO AWAY! DON'T BOTHER! I'M TOO DEPRESSED.

MO ROSE LIMPLY ONTO ONE ELBOW, UNABLE TO ROUSE HIMSELF OUT OF HIS **MOROSE** MOOD.

- Jorge was **morose** after his friend passed away.
- Watching the documentary film about the atrocities of World War II, which contained vivid images of brutal crimes against humanity, the students fell into a **morose** mood.

Indifference

lack of interest or concern; **apathy**, not caring

Think of: **What's the difference?**

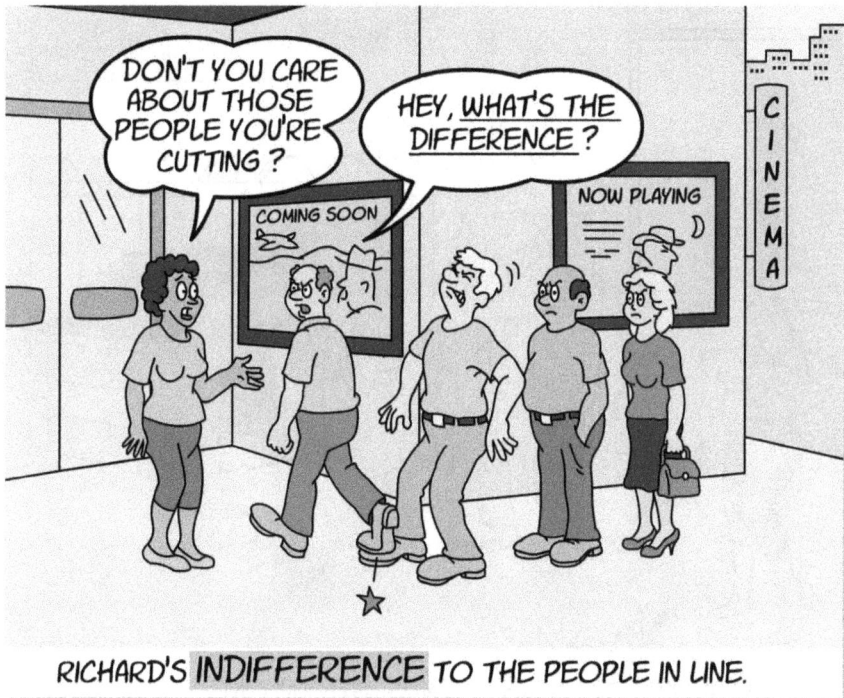

DON'T YOU CARE ABOUT THOSE PEOPLE YOU'RE CUTTING?

HEY, <u>WHAT'S THE DIFFERENCE</u>?

COMING SOON

NOW PLAYING

CINEMA

RICHARD'S **INDIFFERENCE** TO THE PEOPLE IN LINE.

- I am horrified by Richard's **indifference** to the suffering of others.
- Chloe demonstrated her **indifference** to football by drawing sketches in her journal while thousands of rowdy fans cheered around her.

Amiable

friendly, pleasant, agreeable, **congenial**

Think of: **Amy is able**

" AMY IS ABLE TO MAKE FRIENDS WITH ANYONE, BECAUSE SHE IS SO AMIABLE. "

- In their movie roles, the actors Steve Martin and Seth Rogen come across as extremely amiable, because they usually play funny, friendly characters.

- Michael's popularity and abundance of friends are due to his amiable personality; he has none of his brother's sullen, surly tendencies.

Thwart

to oppose successfully, to prevent from accomplishing a purpose, to defeat the efforts of

Think of: **The wart**

- The storm's heavy winds and rain **thwarted** our rescue efforts.
- Our opponent's stifling defense **thwarted** our every attempt to reach the end-zone.

Frugal

practicing economy, avoiding waste, prudently saving or sparing; **thrifty**

Think of: **Rug Al**

RUG AL'S CARPET SHOP WAS SO INEXPENSIVE, THAT THE FRUGAL BUYER COULD BUY RUGS FOR THE ENTIRE HOME FOR UNDER $100.

- What the company needs is a **frugal** money manager who can eliminate excess and waste.
- At many thrift stores, the **frugal** shopper can purchase a new wardrobe – an entire closet full of clothes – for under $100.

Obliterate

to wipe out, erase, or destroy without a trace

Think of: **Obie ate litter**

WHEN *OBIE ATE LITTER*, IT **OBLITERATED** HIS STOMACH.

- When the Iranian President threatened to **obliterate** Israel and erase the country from the map, the world was forced to recognize his country as a threat to peace and stability in the region.

- Faced with extreme budget deficits, the state passed a law which **obliterated** funding for the arts.

1. My friend seemed silent, withdrawn, and _____, which made me wonder what was bothering her so much.

   (A) Florid **(B)** Affable **(C)** Morose **(D)** Amiable **(E)** Frugal

2. The girl was so _____, she purchased all her school supplies for the year on sale for less than $20.

   (A) Florid **(B)** Affable **(C)** Morose **(D)** Amiable **(E)** Frugal

3. The _____ design of the brightly painted poster made it appear cluttered and overly decorated.

   (A) Florid **(B)** Affable **(C)** Morose **(D)** Amiable **(E)** Frugal

4. Because of Joe's _____ personality, he comes across as relaxed, and other people enjoy his company.

   (A) Florid **(B)** Affable **(C)** Morose **(D)** Amiable **(E)** Frugal

5. Tara is gregarious and _____, and so has many friends.

   (A) Florid **(B)** Affable **(C)** Morose **(D)** Amiable **(E)** Frugal

6. Obliterate

   (A) Soothe of pacify **(B)** Speed up **(C)** Criticize or insult
   (D) Support or embrace **(E)** Wipe out or destroy

7. Berate

   (A) Soothe of pacify **(B)** Speed up **(C)** Criticize or insult
   (D) Support or embrace **(E)** Destroy

8. Expedite

   (A) Speed up or hasten **(B)** Hinder or impede **(C)** Mollify or placate
   (D) Ridicule or criticize **(E)** Slow down

9. Indifference

   (A) Apathy or lack of concern **(B)** Difference or gap **(C)** Independence
   (D) Inclination **(E)** Anger or rage

10. Thwart

    (A) Soothe of pacify **(B)** Speed up or hasten **(C)** Criticize or insult
    (D) Support or embrace **(E)** Prevent, suppress, or defeat

Peripheral

located at the outer boundary or edge, not central, of minor importance

Think of: **Purr if fur all**

" THIS CAT WILL ONLY <u>PURR IF</u> THE <u>FUR ALL</u> GETS BRUSHED, NOT JUST THE CENTRAL FUR, BUT THE PERIPHERAL FUR AS WELL. "

- I live in the **peripheral** fringes of the city – the outskirts.
- The teacher tried to refocus the class on the central discussion after students introduced many **peripheral** topics.

Trepidation

fear or nervousness, a state of alarm or dread,
apprehension

Think of: **Trapped nation**

IN A <u>TRAPPED NATION</u>, THE PEOPLE FEEL
MUCH <u>TREPIDATION</u>.

- The frequent gunshots in her neighborhood have left Tina in a state of constant **trepidation**.
- Huddled in the basement, with 120 mile-per-hour winds rattling the house, we felt great **trepidation** as we endured Hurricane Zeno, the 26th of the season.

Erroneous

in error, mistaken, incorrect, wrong

Think of: **Error's on us**

" IF OUR THESIS IS ERRONEOUS, I GUESS THE ERROR'S ON US. "

- Harvey holds the intriguing but **erroneous** belief that the earth is flat.

- Emma's business failed because of some **erroneous** assumptions she made about sales potential.

Dogmatic

asserting opinions in an arrogant, authoritative way; prone to making forcible, unchallengeable assertions; following without questioning

Think of: **Dog's Master**

THE DOG'S MASTER **DOGMATICALLY** ASSERTED THAT HIS WAY WAS THE BEST.

- Joaquin **dogmatically** swore by church doctrine without pausing to question his beliefs or listen to anyone else's.

- Lila's **dogmatic** insistence that her ideas were superior to all others' alienated her friends.

Propensity

an inclination or fondness, a leaning or tendency;
predilection, predisposition, penchant

Think of: **Pro pen city**

Entering
Pro Pen City
Pop: 200,000
" Home of professional writing tools"

THE WORD NERDS AND POETRY GEEKS HAD A PROPENSITY
FOR PRO PEN CITY, A METROPOLIS FULL OF HIGH-QUALITY
WRITING IMPLEMENTS, PERFECT FOR SCRIBBLING THEIR CRAFT.

- She has a **propensity** for knitting sweaters while watching TV.
- The teacher had a **propensity** for incorporating his political views into the curriculum, a tendency which offended some students.

Malicious

harmful, spiteful, vicious, **malevolent**

Think of: **Mal is vicious**

BECAUSE MAL IS SO VICIOUS, THEY SAY HE IS MALICIOUS.

- You are being punished for striking her with **malicious** intent.
- He went to jail for the **malicious** and brutal attack on his roommate.

Malevolent

wishing harm to others, showing ill will; evil, harmful, injurious

Think of: **Mal is violent**

BECAUSE MAL IS VIOLENT, THEY SAY HE IS MALEVOLENT.

- Because of his **malevolent** personality, the con man always plays tricks on people.
- The regime's **malevolent** dictator ordered all music to be banned from the country.

Truncate

to cut off or shorten

Think of: **Trunk ate**

- Because the decimal expansion for the square-root of 2 extends forever, our class decided to **truncate** the number after the 6th digit.

- The emergency was so dire that we were forced to **truncate** the planning period and go right into action. (Note: *dire* = indicating or warning of trouble, disaster, great suffering, or dreadful consequences.)

Rescind

to take back or cancel, to make void, **repeal**, or annul

Think of: **Re-send**

MESSAGES DELETED

NOW THAT MY INTERNET SERVICE PROVIDER HAS RESCINDED EVERY EMAIL I WROTE TODAY, I WILL HAVE TO RESEND THEM.

- The university offered my husband a job but had to **rescind** the offer due to budget cuts.
- It is considered impolite to invite someone to a party and then **rescind** the invitation.

Obstinate

stubborn, hard to control, headstrong

Think of: **Obstacle**

AN *OBSINATE* CHILD IS AN OBSTACLE IN YOUR EFFORTS TO LEAVE THE HOUSE.

- The Governor's **obstinate** refusal to compromise on the tough gun-control legislation paid off when he rallied enough public support to get the new law passed.

- The student's **obstinate** refusal to do any homework was noted by the teacher, who gave him a failing grade.

Review #9

1. The _____ document was full of mistakes and incorrect assumptions.
    (A) Peripheral **(B)** Erroneous **(C)** Dogmatic **(D)** Malicious **(E)** Obstinate

2. His _____ refusal to compromise and stubborn insistence on doing things his own way alienated his friends.
    (A) Peripheral **(B)** Erroneous **(C)** Dogmatic **(D)** Malicious **(E)** Obstinate

3. The teacher asked us to drop all _____ discussions and stay focused on the central lesson of the day.
    (A) Peripheral **(B)** Erroneous **(C)** Dogmatic **(D)** Malicious **(E)** Obstinate

4. I found Joe's insistence that only his own church's religion conveyed the one true word of God to reflect a rather _____ attitude.
    (A) Peripheral **(B)** Erroneous **(C)** Dogmatic **(D)** Malicious **(E)** Obstinate

5. The trick that Tom played on his friends was mean-spirited and _____.
    (A) Peripheral **(B)** Erroneous **(C)** Dogmatic **(D)** Malicious **(E)** Obstinate

6. She had such a _____ for chocolate that she had to consume it three times per day.
    (A) Trepidation **(B)** Propensity **(C)** Indifference **(D)** Iconoclast **(E)** Autonomy

7. Amy was extremely worried and felt much _____ that she would become seriously ill, once so many of her friends got sick.
    (A) Trepidation **(B)** Propensity **(C)** Indifference **(D)** Iconoclast **(E)** Autonomy

8. Malevolent
    (A) Nice or friendly **(B)** Sad or depressed **(C)** Thrifty **(D)** Evil or harmful **(E)** Incorrect or mistaken

9. Truncate
    (A) Take back **(B)** Give away **(C)** Cut off **(D)** Destroy **(E)** Speed up

10. Rescind
    (A) Take back **(B)** Give away **(C)** Cut off **(D)** Destroy **(E)** Speed up

Ignominy

disgrace, shame, or dishonor

Think of: **His name mini**

AFTER THE POLITICIAN FELL INTO IGNOMINY, HIS NAME
BECAME MINI AND DISRESPECTED.

- The politician's reputation fell into **ignominy** after he was convicted of illegal activities, including taking bribes and stealing money from public funds.

- The **ignominy** that has befallen her is due to her own immoral actions.

Deride

to speak of with contempt or ridicule, to mock or make fun of

Think of: **D-ride**

WASN'T THAT AN AWESOME, A + ROLLERCOASTER RIDE ?

NO, I'D SAY IT WAS A D RIDE.

SHE **DERIDES** THE ROLLERCOASTER AND LABELS IT A "D RIDE".

- The parents and teachers **derided** my plan to use PTA funds to provide each student with three cupcakes on every school day.

- The speaker was nervous that the audience would either fall asleep or **deride** his ideas.

Copious

abundant, extensive, **profuse**; full of words and ideas

Think of: **Copy us**

" IF YOU <u>COPY US</u>, WE WILL HAVE A COPIOUS NUMBER
OF DUPLICATE IMAGES. "

- Since I didn't really understand the professor's lecture, I decided to take **copious** notes in class and review them all later for comprehension.

- The **copious**, detailed examples that Jana includes in her essay greatly strengthen her main thesis.

Aberration

a deviation from the norm

Think of: **A Bear Nation**

IN A WORLD OF COUNTRIES CONTROLLED BY HUMAN BEINGS,
A BEAR NATION WOULD BE AN EXTREME ABERRATION.

- Because Jane normally has perfect attendance, her many absences this month represent an **aberration**, which may be a cause for concern.

- The patient's blood pressure has consistently tested normal, so I wonder if this one high reading is just a single **aberration**.

Sedulous

diligent, persevering, **assiduous**, persistent

Think of: **Said you less**

I LOVE HIKING! THIS IS GREAT! YAK, YAK, YAK, YAK!

SAID YOU LESS BUT DID YOU MORE!

ONE CLIMBER MADE A SEDULOUS EFFORT TO REACH THE PEAK OF A MOUNTAIN. HE DIDN'T SAY MUCH ON THE CLIMB. HE JUST DID IT!

- Zack's A+ grades in physics are due to his **sedulous** efforts to complete all assignments and undertake extra credit projects.

- Our **sedulous** attempts to climb the mountain were rewarded when we reached the summit at sunset.

Assiduous

constant in effort or application, working diligently at a task; unceasing, persistent, **sedulous**

Think of: **A's Sid got**

BECAUSE MATH DID NOT COME NATURALLY TO SID, THE <u>A'S SID GOT</u> CAME ONLY AS A RESULT OF HIS ASSIDUOUS STUDIES.

- Sid's **assiduous** effort to do all his history homework and complete a film project for the class enabled him to receive an A.

- After three years of **assiduously** paying every bill on time, Mary was able to restore her credit rating.

Exonerate

to free from blame or guilt, **exculpate**

Think of: **Honor rate**

YOUR HONOR, I HAVE EVIDENCE THAT WILL EXONERATE THE DEFENDANT.

THEN I DO RATE HER NOT GUILTY !

HIS *HONOR RATES* THE DEFENDANT NOT GUILTY AND *EXONERATES* HER OF THE CRIME.

- The actor was accused in court of theft and assault, but a jury ultimately **exonerated** him of the crimes.

- One unfortunate aspect of the death penalty is its finality: if evidence later comes out to **exonerate** the deceased, there is no way to reverse the outcome.

Exculpate

to free from guilt or blame, **exonerate**

Think of: **Ex-culprit**

- There was enough evidence to **exculpate** Toby of the crime.
- The man was **exculpated** when two witnesses came forward to identify the true criminal.

Approbation

approval, commendation, praise; a favorable opinion about someone or something

Think of: **Approval**

SHE RECEIVED THE **APPROBATION** OF HER CLASSMATES BY VOLUNTEERING TO RESCUE THE ENDANGERED FROGS FROM THE SEWER SYSTEM.

- Laura won **approbation** from her classmates for rescuing the endangered frogs.
- The professor has earned **approbation** for his humanitarian relief work and AIDS research.

Hubris

excessive pride, overbearing arrogance

Think of: **You breeze**

WHY DON'T YOU HIKE UP THIS MOUNTAIN THE EASY WAY? THAT'S THE SLOW WAY TO GO!

A PERSON WHO THINKS <u>YOU</u> CAN <u>BREEZE</u> THROUGH EVERYTHING IN LIFE MAY BE SUFFERING FROM HUBRIS.

- When the arrogant rock star claimed to be the greatest guitarist ever, music critics derided his **hubris**. (Note: to deride = to ridicule, mock, or make fun of)

- In ancient Greek drama, characters who committed acts of **hubris** by comparing themselves to the gods were ultimately punished for their arrogance.

1. The mythological character named Icarus, who used a pair of wings to escape Crete, arrogantly thought he could fly all the way to the sun, but his _____ was punished by a great fall to the sea when the wax holding his wings melted.

   (A) Ignominy **(B)** Aberration **(C)** Hubris **(D)** Propensity **(E)** Trepidation

2. Ed is usually a great sprinter who places within the top 10% of any field, so his last place performance in today's race can be considered an _____.

   (A) Ignominy **(B)** Aberration **(C)** Autonomy **(D)** Approbation **(E)** Irony

3. There is no shame or _____ in being arrested while defending a just cause; some of the world's greatest leaders have been arrested in defense of a firmly held belief.

   (A) Ignominy **(B)** Aberration **(C)** Approbation **(D)** Hubris **(E)** Propensity

4. Amy received much _____ and several awards for her work helping humanity and cleaning up the polluted city.

   (A) Ignominy **(B)** Aberration **(C)** Approbation **(D)** Hubris **(E)** Indifference

5. Deride

   (A) Take back **(B)** Make fun of **(C)** Speed up **(D)** Free from blame
   (E) Cut short

6. Copious

   (A) Abundant **(B)** Lacking **(C)** Diligent **(D)** Mistaken **(E)** Harmful

7. Sedulous

   (A) Abundant **(B)** Lacking **(C)** Evil or vicious **(D)** Stubborn **(E)** Diligent

8. Assiduous

   (A) Bitter **(B)** Not central **(C)** Abundant **(D)** Stubborn **(E)** Sedulous

9. Exonerate

   (A) Go backwards, decline **(B)** Speed up **(C)** Repeal **(D)** Free from blame
   (E) Destroy

10. Exculpate

    (A) Remove from blame **(B)** Find guilty **(C)** Cut short **(D)** Take back
    (E) Mock or ridicule

Apathetic

not interested, not caring, unconcerned, **indifferent**

Think of: **A.P. athletics**

- The teacher noted, "While Ann is interested and motivated in class, Bob is, unfortunately, **apathetic**."

- Sadly, some people remain **apathetic** even when witnessing the suffering of others.

Pragmatic

pertaining to practical considerations

Think of: **Practical**

DANA HAS A **PRAGMATIC** APPROACH TO SAVING MONEY.
SHE IS <u>PRACTICAL</u> AND COLLECTS ALL HER SPARE CHANGE
IN ONE GIANT PIGGY BANK.

- Even though we were late for the concert, we made the **pragmatic** decision to stop for gas.

- As a computer programmer, Matt is very **pragmatic**; he borrows and incorporates software from many sources, rather than having to rewrite every program himself.

Serendipitous

lucky in making unexpected and fortunate discoveries; **fortuitous**, favorable

Think of: **Sarah's dip**

SARAH'S DIP WAS SERENDIPITOUS, BECAUSE SHE DID NOT EXPECT TO FIND THE HIDDEN LAKE IN THE MOUNTAINS, JUST WHEN SHE WAS SO HOT AND EXHAUSTED.

- Sarah made the **serendipitous** discovery of a hidden mountain spring just when she was hot and exhausted from the arduous hike.
- To stumble into a café late at night only to find your favorite band playing there would be **serendipitous**.

Fortuitous

happening by chance, accidental, lucky, fortunate

Think of: **Fort Two it is**

- How **fortuitous** that you drove up and offered me a ride, just when I was caught in the rain without an umbrella.

- The baseball manager's decision to rest his all-star pitcher in game six was **fortuitous**: when game seven went to extra innings, he suddenly found himself in need of the pitching ace.

Indigenous

native to an area, originating and occurring naturally in a particular region

Think of: **Dig in**

THE **INDIGENOUS** PEOPLE OF NORTH AMERICA WERE THE FIRST TO DIG INTO THE LAND, LONG BEFORE EUROPEAN COLONISTS ARRIVED.

- Native Americans are often referred to as the **indigenous** people of the Americas, because they lived on the continent for centuries before Europeans arrived.

- While most bamboos are native to Asia, there are a few species **indigenous** to the United States, such as "river cane" bamboo, **indigenous** to the Appalachian region.

Supplant

to take the place of by force, strategy, or scheming; to displace or replace

Think of: **Super plant**

THE SUPER PLANTS WERE ABLE TO SUPPLANT ALL INDIGENOUS PLANT SPECIES AND DISPLACE THE REGION'S NATIVE FLORA.

- In 2011, democratic activists in Syria took to the streets in an effort to **supplant** the oppressive regime controlling their country.

- The Monterey Pine is native to a limited section of the California coast. The tree acts as an aggressor outside this region, **supplanting** indigenous plant species.

Haughty

arrogant, disdainful, proud, snobbish

Think of: **Height of T**

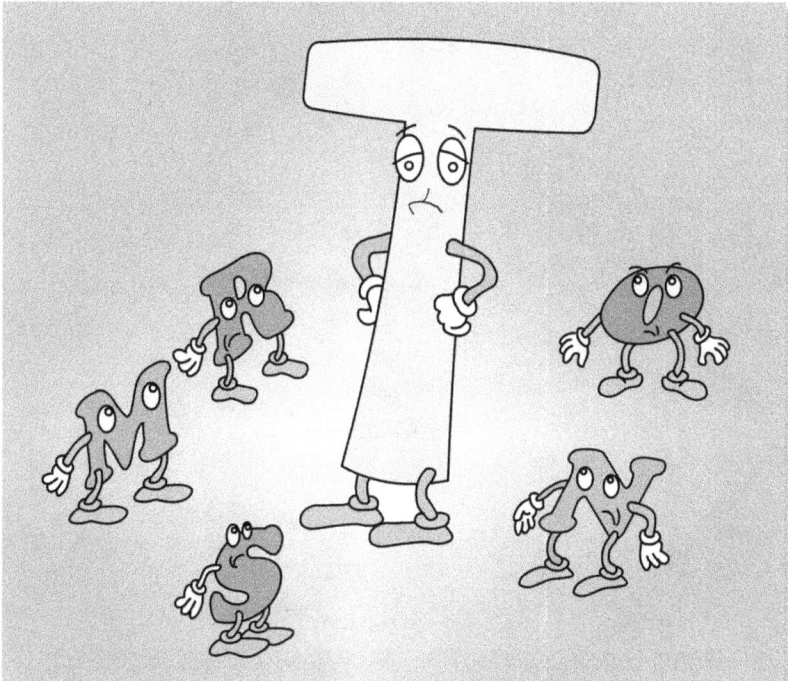

THE <u>HEIGHT OF T</u> GAVE THE IMPRESSION THAT HE WAS
HAUGHTY AND LOOKED DOWN ON THE OTHERS.

- The **haughty** princess rarely condescends to speak to mere commoners.

- While many celebrities are down-to-earth and accessible, others come across as extremely **haughty**.

Eclectic

selecting or drawing from many sources, combining elements from various sources

Think of: **E collects ticks**

BECAUSE <u>E COLLECTS TICKS</u> AND MANY OTHER INSECTS, HE IS KNOWN FOR HIS **ECLECTIC** BUG COLLECTION.

- Shannon has **eclectic** taste in music, enjoying anything from classical flute, to hip-hop, to fusion jazz.

- Zack's **eclectic** collection of sports memorabilia includes old baseball cards, hockey pucks, golf tees from the Ryder Cup, and even sweat socks worn in the Super Bowl.

Indecorous

not following proper decorum or rules of behavior, violating accepted standards of good taste and propriety

Think of: **Indie core us**

OUR INDECOROUS BEHAVIOR IS ATTRIBUTABLE TO OUR INDIE CORE, OUR INDEPENDENT SPIRIT.

- At a fancy wedding banquet, it would be **indecorous** to eat with your hands.
- The traditional husband criticized his wife for what he called "improper manners and **indecorous** behavior."

Adhere

to support or follow a cause, to stick fast or stay attached

Think of: **Ad here**

THIS SPACE AVAILABLE
PLACE YOUR AD HERE.
OUR SUPER GLUE WILL
ENSURE THAT YOUR
AD HERE WILL ADHERE
TO THE BILLBOARD.

- Monks and nuns are thought to **adhere** to a strict, religious lifestyle.
- An epoxy is a powerful type of glue used to make metals and other materials **adhere** to each other.

1. Wild lions are now _____ mainly to the savannas of Africa, although, until about 10,000 years ago, they were the most widespread large land mammal other than humans.

    (A) Apathetic **(B)** Pragmatic **(C)** Serendipitous **(D)** Fortuitous **(E)** Indigenous

2. Her _____ manners at the wedding included eating with her hands and walking on the table.

    (A) Haughty **(B)** Eclectic **(C)** Indecorous **(D)** Pragmatic **(E)** Serendipitous

3. Lucy's illness has made her _____: she lies in bed all day, with no interest in eating, reading, or even watching TV.

    (A) Apathetic **(B)** Eclectic **(C)** Haughty **(D)** Fortuitous **(E)** Indigenous

4. Jesse's wide-ranging CD collection, which includes many jazz, rap, and rock albums, is testament to his _____ taste in music.

    (A) Serendipitous **(B)** Eclectic **(C)** Haughty **(D)** Indecorous **(E)** Fortuitous

5. It was _____ that my other client cancelled her lesson just when you were so desperate to get into my schedule for a lesson before the final.

    (A) Fortuitous **(B)** Eclectic **(C)** Haughty **(D)** Apathetic **(E)** Indigenous

6. Her decision to choose the local community college was _____: by living at home, she will save on expenses and be able to afford her college education.

    (A) Apathetic **(B)** Serendipitous **(C)** Eclectic **(D)** Pragmatic **(E)** Indecorous

7. Serendipitous

    (A) Terrifying **(B)** Arrogant or snobbish **(C)** Ill-tempered
    (D) Fortuitous or favorable **(E)** Native to an area

8. Supplant

    (A) Hide discreetly **(B)** Take the place of **(C)** Inspect thoroughly
    (D) Follow or listen to **(E)** Demolish or destroy

9. Haughty

    (A) Using bad manners **(B)** Practical **(C)** Not interested, not caring
    (D) Lucky or favorable **(E)** Arrogant or proud

10. Adhere

    (A) Tout or promote **(B)** Support or follow a cause **(C)** Replace or displace
    (D) Harm or injure **(E)** Criticize

Heinous

hateful, reprehensible, odious, abominable

Think of: **Hate us**

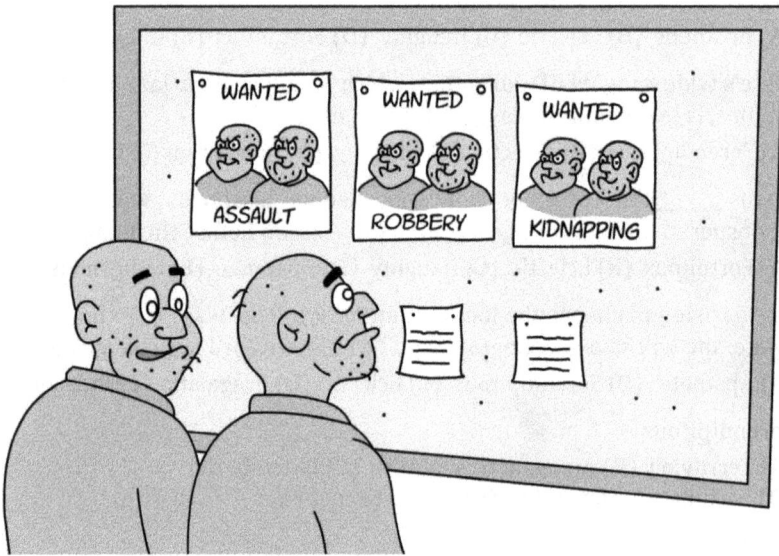

" BECAUSE WE COMMIT SO MANY *HEINOUS* ACTS, PEOPLE HATE US. "

- The **heinous** crimes committed by former Cambodian dictator Pol Pot have been well-documented.
- The massacre of innocent civilians in Somalia and the brutal actions of Mexican drug gangs are evidence that **heinous** acts continue to be committed worldwide.

Trivial

minor or unimportant, of little value or significance

Think of: **Trial vial**

THE TRIAL VIALS CONTAINED A **TRIVIAL** AMOUNT OF PERFUME, MAKING IT FRUSTRATINGLY HARD TO SAMPLE THE SCENTS.

- Ed thought his idea was original and powerful, but I found it rather **trivial**.

- Attempts by the conservative media to brand *Occupy Wall Street* protesters as "drug-using hippies" represent a concerted effort to **trivialize** the real concerns that the protesters have.

Undermine

to weaken or cause to collapse by removing underlying support, to injure or destroy by insidious activity or indirect means

Think of: **Mine under**

BY DIGGING A <u>MINE UNDER</u> THE PEACE MARCH, THE MILITANTS **UNDERMINED** THE PEACE PROCESS.

- The high-level peace talks in Geneva, which seemed to be making progress, were **undermined** by fighting on the ground.
- By playing with sand in the house while I clean up, you are **undermining** my cleaning efforts.

Skeptical

having or showing doubt; questioning or denying

Think of: **Skip tackle**

- A good scientist should remain **skeptical** of any new theory until there is substantial evidence of the theory's validity.

- The woman is **skeptical** of the suggestion that the Environmental Protection Agency can be eliminated and that companies would self-regulate their own pollution.

Hierarchy

any system of people or things ranked one above another

Think of: **Higher arch**

BY BUILDING A <u>HIGHER ARCH</u>, A MIDDLE ARCH, AND A LOWER ARCH, THE ARCHITECT CREATED A **HIERARCHY** OF FANS ENTERING THE COLISEUM.

- I don't like working for that company because of the **hierarchy**: those at the top make all the decisions and money, while those at the bottom receive little recognition and few benefits.

- To become the Pope, a Christian must spend years ascending the **hierarchy** of the Catholic Church before reaching the top.

Superfluous

excessive, extra, **extraneous**; more than necessary or required

Think of: **Super fluids**

- When the billionaire founder of a company won the lottery, the two-million dollar prize was **superfluous** to his existing wealth, so he donated it charity.

- Our mature apple tree already provides hundreds more apples per year than we could possibly eat, so planting a second tree would be **superfluous**.

Cursory

going rapidly over something without noticing details, hasty and **superficial**

Think of: **Curse story**

" OF COURSE SHE WILL <u>CURSE</u> THE <u>STORY</u>. SHE'S GIVING IT SUCH A CURSORY READ, SHE CAN'T POSSIBLY GLEAN ANY OF THE MEANING. "

- I didn't have time to read the full report, but I gave it a **cursory** look and noted the main findings.
- Even a **cursory** scan of his face revealed the depression he was suffering.

Boisterous

noisy, rowdy, unrestrained, unruly, **clamorous**

Think of: **Boys stir us**

- The **boisterous** wedding celebration could be heard throughout the town, late into the night.
- Jose has a **boisterous** personality – he is loud, outgoing, and emphatic.

Impede

to obstruct progress or movement by means of obstacles and hindrances; **hinder**, **hamper**.

Think of: **Imp eats**

WHEN THE <u>IMP EATS</u>, IT IMPEDES ALL PROGRESS IN THE KITCHEN.

- Your lack of cooperation is **impeding** our progress.
- The dry weather and high winds have **impeded** the firefighters' efforts to contain the conflagration.

Hinder

to obstruct or get in the way of; to cause delay, interruption, or difficulty; **hamper**, **impede**

Think of: **Hinter**

SEE THAT GUY ? I'LL GIVE YOU A HINT. HE MAY BE INVOLVED IN THE MURDER.

A <u>HINTER</u> WILL **HINDER** YOUR ENJOYMENT OF THE MOVIE.

- Another week of storms will **hinder** the construction project and further delay its completion.
- The deep snow blanketing the roads **hindered** our progress home from the mountains.

1. The party was a rowdy and _____ celebration that could be heard throughout the village.

   (A) Heinous **(B)** Trivial **(C)** Skeptical **(D)** Cursory **(E)** Boisterous

2. Jane had no time to study properly for the test and could only give the notes a _____ glance.

   (A) Trivial **(B)** Superfluous **(C)** Skeptical **(D)** Cursory **(E)** Boisterous

3. Even though Jason loved baseball, he found the gift of baseball cards to be _____ because he already owned a complete set of cards, and the ones in the gift duplicated ones he already owned.

   (A) Heinous **(B)** Superfluous **(C)** Skeptical **(D)** Cursory **(E)** Boisterous

4. In the 1930s and '40s, the German chancellor, Adolph Hitler, committed _____ crimes against humanity, including murder and torture.

   (A) Heinous **(B)** Superfluous **(C)** Trivial **(D)** Cursory **(E)** Boisterous

5. Even though it is crucial to tackle the major environmental problems threatening our planet as a whole, we should not consider _____ any individual community's wish to clean its own local environment.

   (A) Heinous **(B)** Superfluous **(C)** Trivial **(D)** Cursory **(E)** Skeptical

6. I believe many players on the Wizards to be extremely talented, so I am _____ of Zoe's claim to be "the best on the team by far."

   (A) Heinous **(B)** Superfluous **(C)** Trivial **(D)** Boisterous **(E)** Skeptical

7. Undermine

   (A) Weaken or cause to collapse **(B)** Displace **(C)** Follow or stick to **(D)** Dig or burrow **(E)** Castigate or rebuke

8. Hierarchy

   (A) Opulent mansion **(B)** Lack of interest **(C)** Excessive pride **(D)** Ranked or tiered system **(E)** Rowdy or noisy celebration

9. Impede

   (A) Obstruct or hinder **(B)** Find and destroy **(C)** Rebuke or chastise **(D)** Hide or sequester **(E)** Free from blame, exculpate

10. Hinder

    (A) Free from blame **(B)** Cut short or reduce **(C)** Honor or restrict **(D)** Obstruct or get in the way of **(E)** Deride or scorn

Proficient

skilled, competent; having an advanced degree of competence in an art, profession, or branch of learning

Think of: **Pro fisher**

A PRO FISHER MUST BE *PROFICIENT* AT CATCHING FISH.

- Ann is a **proficient** tennis player and competes against nationally ranked opponents.

- While Ed has no musical talent, he is a **proficient** painter and writer.

Disgruntled

displeased and discontented, feeling anger or resentment

Think of: **Grunt**

AS THEY PERFORMED THEIR MENIAL TASKS, THE DISGRUNTLED FARM WORKERS GRUNTED AS MUCH AS THE HOGS WHOSE PENS THEY HAD TO CLEAN.

- Many of the nation's young people, **disgruntled** by the lack of opportunities and a gaping disparity of wealth in society, participated in the Occupy movement.

- When Syrian leader Assad agreed to reforms at an Arab League summit, but immediately sent his tanks to attack peaceful protestors, the Syrian people felt **disgruntled**.

Sanguine

cheerfully optimistic, hopeful, confident

Think of: **Gwen sang**

GWEN SANG ALL DAY LONG BECAUSE SHE WAS SO SANGUINE ABOUT THE STATE OF THE WORLD AND HER LIFE.

- Many people remain **sanguine** about our country's future, despite all the problems and challenges we face.

- Marcus felt **sanguine** about his chances of getting an A in math after scoring a 99 on the recent test.

Empirical

derived from observation or experiment rather than theory

Think of: **Umpire**

THE UMPIRE'S DECISION IS EMPIRICAL; HE HAS TO CALL THE PLAY BASED ON HIS DIRECT OBSERVATION.

- The theory of quantum mechanics, which makes predictions about electrons and other very small particles, has been confirmed by an overwhelming amount of **empirical** evidence.

- While the new scientific theories are intriguing, they have not yet been verified by **empirical** observations.

Furtive

secretive, **stealthy**, **surreptitious**

Think of: **Fur thief**

A FUR THIEF MUST BE FURTIVE WHEN CASING THE STORE.

- While trying to sneak out of the store with a shiny new iPod, the thief kept glancing **furtively** at the store's security guards.

- At Mel's Diner, the shy boy cast a **furtive** glance from behind a menu at the pretty girl at the end of the counter.

Extol

to praise, commend, **laud, adulate**

Think of: **Exit toll**

" OF COURSE I **EXTOL** THE EXIT TOLL, BECAUSE OUR
STATE NEEDS THE MONEY FOR ROAD IMPROVEMENT. "

- I **extol** the virtues of honesty, integrity, and loyalty.
- The teacher **extolled** Annika for her dedication, perseverance, and hard work.

Juxtapose

to place side by side for the purposes of comparison

Think of: **Just a pose**

COME ON, STAND NEXT TO EACH OTHER FOR JUST A MOMENT, JUST A POSE.

THE PHOTOGRAPHER JUXTAPOSES THE ANGEL AND DEVIL, JUST FOR ONE POSE.

- When the professor **juxtaposed** the facts of the election in the U.S. between Tilden and Hayes in 1876, with those of the Bush-Gore election in 2000, he noticed striking similarities.

- **Juxtaposed** with the poor neighborhood surrounding it, the new corporate headquarters of Company X is a jarring display of opulence.

Surfeit

an excess or excessive amount, an abundance of food or drink

Think of: **Surf it**

THIS BEACH HAS A SURFEIT OF LARGE, EXCITING WAVES TODAY.

ARE YOU GOING TO SURF IT?

SURFBOARD RENTALS

- The **surfeit** of long rolling waves at Tamarindo Beach, Costa Rica, makes surfers from all over the world want to surf it.
- The party included a **surfeit** of food and drink.

Hiatus

a break or gap in continuity or time, an interruption in a schedule

Think of: **Hyatt us**

- After a four-week Christmas **hiatus** spent entirely at a luxury resort, the professors had a hard time getting back to the rigors of a new academic semester.
- There has been a three-day **hiatus** in negotiations for the holiday.

Feasible

capable of being done, achieved, or effected; possible

Think of: **Fees enable**

- In an effort to reduce the use of cars downtown, the city conducted a study to determine whether the construction of a new subway would be **feasible**.

- While the goal of universal college education is noble and desirable, many people argue that it is not **feasible** for the federal government to pay everyone's way.

Review #13

1. Jen is a/an _____ musician who can play three different instruments and sing adeptly.

    (A) Proficient **(B)** Disgruntled **(C)** Sanguine **(D)** Empirical **(E)** Furtive

2. The prisoner made a/an _____ attempt to sneak past the guards and escape the jail.

    (A) Proficient **(B)** Disgruntled **(C)** Prominent **(D)** Empirical **(E)** Furtive

3. The postal workers felt _____ when their salary and benefits were drastically reduced.

    (A) Elated **(B)** Disgruntled **(C)** Feasible **(D)** Empirical **(E)** Furtive

4. Despite the temporary setback in negotiations, analysts are _____ that peace can be achieved in the region.

    (A) Proficient **(B)** Disgruntled **(C)** Feasible **(D)** Sanguine **(E)** Furtive

5. Although there is an elegant beauty to String Theory, which posits that everything in the universe arises from incredibly small strings of energy which vibrate at various frequencies, there is still no _____ evidence to confirm the theory.

    (A) Proficient **(B)** Disgruntled **(C)** Sanguine **(D)** Empirical **(E)** Furtive

6. I find your plan for ending poverty to be admirable but impractical; although the goal is noble, it's not _____ to implement your idea.

    (A) Proficient **(B)** Disgruntled **(C)** Feasible **(D)** Empirical **(E)** Furtive

7. Extol

    (A) Laud or acclaim **(B)** Place side by side **(C)** Denigrate or degrade
    (D) Weaken or cause to collapse **(E)** Hamper or impede

8. Juxtapose

    (A) Malign or deride **(B)** Place side by side for purposes of comparison
    (C) Praise **(D)** Delay or postpone **(E)** Free from blame; exonerate or exculpate

9. Surfeit

    (A) Dearth or meager supply **(B)** Break in time or continuity
    (C) Abundance or excess amount **(D)** A system based on rank or order
    (E) Lack of interest or concern

10. Hiatus

    (A) Abundance or excess amount **(B)** Dearth or meager supply
    (C) Dishonor or shame **(D)** Inclination, preference, or tendency
    (E) A break or gap in continuity or time

Provincial

1. lacking urban sophistication or broadmindedness; limited in perspective; unsophisticated, narrow-minded
2. belonging to or related to a province

Think of: **Prove insular** (Note: insular = isolated, detached.)

- Howard's views on the matter are rather **provincial** and demonstrate a lack of awareness of the issues.

- The sophisticated urbanite somewhat snobbishly dismissed the visitor's opinions as **provincial**.

Sporadic

occurring at irregular intervals, occasional

Think of: **Sports addict**

- It rained **sporadically** throughout the night.
- Because Eric is physically fit and healthy, his visits to the doctor have become **sporadic**.

Intractable

difficult to deal with or solve; difficult to work with or control

Think of: **Not tractor-able**

THE LAND IS SO **INTRACTABLE**, IT IS NOT DIG-ABLE AND NOT TRACTOR-ABLE.

- My friend joined a support group for people suffering from **intractable** pain.

- Some analysts believe that the crisis in the Middle East is **intractable**.

Innate

existing in one from birth; inborn, inherent

Think of: **Inner nature**

- Dogs have the **innate** ability to recognize many more distinct scents than humans can.

- Many people believe that running speed is an **innate** gift, but great sprinters know that intense training is also required to achieve fleetness of foot.

Abridge

to shorten, cut short, or reduce

Think of: **A bridge**

"SINCE <u>A BRIDGE</u> WAS BUILT BETWEEN TRAIL A AND TRAIL B, THE DISTANCE HAS BEEN ABRIDGED FROM 12 MILES TO 200 METERS."

- The natural rights of humans to life, liberty, and the pursuit of happiness shall not be **abridged**.

- The couple had to **abridge** their honeymoon when the bride's father became deathly ill.

Avarice

insatiable greed, a desire to hoard wealth

Think of: **Available rice**

THE NATO RELIEF TRUCK ALMOST GOT THROUGH, BUT WE HIJACKED IT.

GREAT WORK !

THE MILITARY DICTATOR'S **AVARICE** IS SEEN IN HIS DECISION TO HOARD ALL OF THE COUNTRY'S <u>AVAILABLE RICE</u>.

- Full of **avarice**, the man was not content with his fortune and destroyed the lives of his friends to make even more money.

- In fiction, the character who typifies **avarice** is Ebenezer Scrooge – from Charles Dickens's novel, *A Christmas Carol* – who is a cold-hearted, tight-fisted miser.

Abhor

to hate, detest, or loathe

Think of: **Horror**

- Since Julie **abhors** horror movies, Ryan's decision to take her to the gruesome monster flick did not go over well.

- Hannah **abhors** the chores that her mother gives her.

Diffident

timid, shy, lacking confidence

Think of: **Different dent**

I DON'T THINK I CAUSED THAT DENT

WHEN MAYA BACKED INTO THE NEW CAR, SHE WAS DIFFIDENT ABOUT ADMITTING RESPONSIBILITY, SUGGESTING IT WAS A DIFFERENT DENT.

- The **diffident** girl had the habit of repeatedly saying, "I'm sorry," and apologizing for every action.

- Many people feel **diffident** about having to speak in public in a language that is not their native tongue.

Arduous

hard, difficult, tiring, requiring physical exertion

Think of: **Hard for you and us**

"AN **ARDUOUS** HIKE UP THE MOUNTAIN IS <u>HARD</u> <u>FOR YOU AND US</u>."

- The boys threw down their backpacks and crashed on the ground after an **arduous** hike up the mountain.

- In the movie, *Star Wars*, Luke Skywalker must undertake an **arduous** journey before confronting Darth Vader.

Condone

to pardon or forgive, to disregard an offense, to give tacit approval

Think of: **Convict done**

WE SHOULD CONDONE THE CRIMES OF A CONVICT WHO HAS DONE HIS TIME.

- It is only fair to **condone** the crimes of a person who has already served an appropriate prison sentence for those crimes.

- The teacher **condoned** the student's bad behavior one time only, warning the child that further aggression toward others would be punished with removal from the class.

1. The coach believes that great athletic ability is _____: it can't be taught, you have to be born with it.
    (A) Provincial **(B)** Sporadic **(C)** Intractable **(D)** Innate **(E)** Diffident

2. People who grow up in rural areas and who are not exposed to worldly, multi-cultural perspectives are in danger of developing _____ points of view.
    (A) Provincial **(B)** Arduous **(C)** Intractable **(D)** Innate **(E)** Diffident

3. I had hoped for consistently good weather on our vacation in Hawaii, but the appearance of the sun was only _____, and most of the time it rained.
    (A) Provincial **(B)** Arduous **(C)** Sporadic **(D)** Innate **(E)** Intractable

4. Joe is so _____, he timidly hid in his room throughout the entire party.
    (A) Provincial **(B)** Arduous **(C)** Sporadic **(D)** Innate **(E)** Diffident

5. The fantasy movie's hero faced an incredibly _____ journey, in which he had to cross the barren Plain of Trolls and scale the Wasted Mountains before facing the dragons.
    (A) Provincial **(B)** Arduous **(C)** Intractable **(D)** Sporadic **(E)** Diffident

6. The negotiations between the two groups have become _____; few people believe that the deadlock will ever be resolved.
    (A) Innate **(B)** Arduous **(C)** Intractable **(D)** Sporadic **(E)** Diffident

7. Abridge
    (A) Reduce or shorten **(B)** Prolong or extend **(C)** Pardon or forgive
    (D) Laud or praise **(E)** Harm or impair

8. Avarice
    (A) Anger **(B)** Greed **(C)** Abundance **(D)** Interruption **(E)** Benevolence

9. Abhor
    (A) Annoy **(B)** Love **(C)** Hate **(D)** Embellish **(E)** Discard

10. Condone
    (A) Blame **(B)** Attack **(C)** Appease **(D)** Avoid **(E)** Forgive

Docile

obedient, tame, easy to control or manage

Think of: **Dogs' isle**

THE DOGS ARE ALL **DOCILE** ON <u>DOGS' ISLE</u>.

- A tame dog is even more **docile** after a good meal.
- Cows are **docile** animals: easily-herded, gentle herbivores.

Itinerant

traveling from place to place, especially for work

Think of: **A tiny ant**

A TINY ANT CAN BE THOUGHT OF AS ITINERANT BECAUSE IT NEVER STOPS MOVING.

- The **itinerant** farm workers drove from ranch to ranch looking for jobs as fruit pickers or field laborers.

- Ramon's new career has forced him into an **itinerant** lifestyle; he travels across the continent for conferences at least twice per week.

Inundate

to flood or cover with water, to overwhelm

Think of: **Inn under water**

FLOOD WATERS INUNDATED THE TOWN, SO THE HISTORIC INN WAS UNDER WATER.

- I'd love to come to the movies with you, but I'm **inundated** with homework.

- Three straight weeks of heavy rain has left the river swollen and the town **inundated**.

Abash

to make someone feel embarrassed or ashamed

Think of: **A rash**

EMMA FELT TOO **ABASHED** TO LEAVE THE HOUSE
BECAUSE OF A RASH.

- Would you be too **abashed** to go out in public if you had rash covering your face?

- Sadly, the boy hated to be seen with his parents, who would **abash** him in front of his friends.

Abstruse

difficult to understand, obscure

Think of: **Abstract truths**

THE ACCELERATION OF AN OBJECT IS DIRECTLY PROPORTIONAL TO THE NET FORCE ACTING ON THE OBJECT AND INVERSELY PROPORTIONAL TO ITS MASS.

ABSTRACT TRUTHS ARE ABSTRUSE.

- Even the advanced graduate students found the professor's lecture on 6-dimensional topology to be rather **abstruse**.

- Many young English scholars find the writings of James Joyce to be highly **abstruse** and filled with cryptic references. (Note: *cryptic* = mysterious, puzzling)

Scrutinize

to study carefully or examine in detail

Think of: **Screw in eyes**

" AFTER I TOOK THE TIME TO SCRUTINIZE YOUR STOREFRONT SIGN, I DECIDED IT WOULD BE MORE EFFECTIVE IF I SCREW IN THESE EYES. "

- Religious scholars **scrutinize** the Bible, looking for patterns and deeper messages.

- In some countries, it is important to **scrutinize** the bill in a restaurant, because there may be extraneous charges intended to bilk unwary foreigners. (Notes: *bilk* = swindle; *unwary* = unaware or not cautious.)

Meticulous

extremely careful and precise; painstakingly attentive to details

Think of: **Me tireless**

- The stage designers paid **meticulous** attention to every detail in recreating an 18th Century French parlor room for the set of the play.

- The automobile-making company, Ford, sought to rebuild its reputation by **meticulously** engineering every component of its new cars.

Ambiguous

open to several interpretations, vague, unclear in meaning, **equivocal**

Think of: **Am big user**

I AM A BIG USER OF STEROIDS.

ALTHOUGH HIS LAWYER ADVISED HIM TO GIVE AN **AMBIGUOUS** RESPONSE TO REPORTERS, THE WEIGHT-LIFTER MADE AN **UNAMBIGUOUS** CONFESSION.

- The politician's **ambiguous** answer on the issue of funding for education caused his advocates to question their support.

- When James asked Liz to the prom, she gave an **ambiguous** reply and kept him waiting for two weeks before responding definitively.

Exacerbate

to make worse, aggravate, irritate, or increase the severity

Think of: **Excess Serb ate**

SERB THOUGHT THAT EATING SIX BOWLS OF CHICKEN SOUP
WOULD MAKE HIM FEEL BETTER, BUT THE <u>EXCESS SERB</u>
<u>ATE</u> ONLY EXACERBATED HIS ILLNESS.

- Far from solving the crisis, the new law will only **exacerbate** the situation.

- Trying to "walk off" a broken leg will **exacerbate** the injury, because the broken bone, when moved, may damage nearby muscles and ligaments.

Inert

inactive, not moving, not reactive

Think of: **Insert**

- We expected the bats to become active at dusk, but they remained **inert** until nightfall.
- The woman felt so **inert** on the couch, with her new book and the cat curled up on her lap, that she summoned her children to fetch her water and snacks.

Review #15

1. I liked the ideas in Lou's essay, but his thesis was ___; I could not clearly tell which side of the issue he was taking.
   (A) Docile **(B)** Itinerant **(C)** Meticulous **(D)** Inert **(E)** Ambiguous

2. Neon is called an ____ gas, because it is chemically unreactive and rarely combines or reacts with other elements.
   (A) Intractable **(B)** Itinerant **(C)** Abstruse **(D)** Inert **(E)** Ambiguous

3. Don't worry, that dog is ___ and won't bite.
   (A) Docile **(B)** Itinerant **(C)** Abstruse **(D)** Ambiguous **(E)** Meticulous

4. The _____ fisherman has been migrating up and down the coast, visiting small fishing villages, moving wherever there's work.
   (A) Docile **(B)** Itinerant **(C)** Ambiguous **(D)** Inert **(E)** Meticulous

5. In cleaning the apartment, the professional janitorial company paid _____ attention to detail and diligently cleaned every spot.
   (A) Abstruse **(B)** Itinerant **(C)** Docile **(D)** Inert **(E)** Meticulous

6. Many people love author Thomas Pynchon's creative, abstract novels, but to truly understand his ___ writing requires dedication and concentration.
   (A) Abstruse **(B)** Itinerant **(C)** Docile **(D)** Inert **(E)** Meticulous

7. Inundate
   (A) Make worse **(B)** Improve **(C)** Retreat **(D)** Discern or decipher
   (E) Flood or cover with water

8. Abash
   (A) Study carefully **(B)** Hide or conceal **(C)** Embarrass
   (D) Come together or unite **(E)** Waver or fluctuate

9. Scrutinize
   (A) Intimidate **(B)** Reduce in severity, lessen the pain **(C)** Study carefully
   (D) Trigger or incite **(E)** Rebel

10. Exacerbate
    (A) Reduce in severity, lessen the pain **(B)** Make worse **(C)** Nullify or cancel
    (D) Exonerate, free from blame **(E)** Create confusion

Indolent

lazy, **lethargic**; not showing interest, effort, or energy

Think of: **In dull land**

IN DULL LAND, THE COUCH POTATOES FEEL INDOLENT
AND MAKE NO EFFORT TO DO ANYTHING.

- That **indolent** man has never worked a day in his life.
- The boss knew that Tina was dishonest, but hired her anyway because he was too **indolent** to care and too lazy to interview other candidates.

Perilous

involving danger, risk, or hazard; dangerous

Think of: **Peer less**

BECAUSE WE <u>PEER LESS</u> AT WHERE WE'RE GOING, OUR
RUN ACROSS THE MINE FIELD IS MORE **PERILOUS.**

- The soldier's dash across the minefield was extremely **perilous**.
- The ship's captain set a **perilous** course through the eye of the storm.

Impasse

a point from which no progress can be made; a deadlock, stalemate, or standoff

Think of: **Impossible to pass**

IT IS <u>IMPOSSIBLE TO PASS</u>, ONCE AN **IMPASSE** IS REACHED.

- The peace negotiations reached an **impasse**, with neither side willing to compromise.

- Because 400 million dollars separated the two sides, the collective bargaining **impasse** could not be easily solved.

Antithetical

diametrically or directly opposed, expressing the exact opposite

Think of: **Auntie theatrical**

- To spend government money freely and liberally on unproven programs is **antithetical** to Bill's philosophy as a fiscal conservative.

- To steal our classmate's spot on the line would be **antithetical** to the spirit of trust and teamwork that the school is trying to foster. (Note: *foster* = to nurture or promote the development of.)

Ebullient

full of cheerful excitement or enthusiasm, high-spirited or bubbly, overflowing with zeal or enthusiasm, **exuberant**

Think of: **E bubbly**

BECAUSE E IS SO BUBBLY WITH EXCITEMENT AT BEING THE MOST COMMON VOWEL, THE OTHER LETTERS SAY HE'S EBULLIENT.

- The teenagers were in an **ebullient** mood at the rock concert and were quickly energized by the music.
- The actress felt **ebullient** to be onstage holding her Oscar statuette, having just won the coveted Academy Award.

Cynical

believing that people are motivated mainly by selfish concerns, distrustful of human nature or motives

Think of: **See nickel**

A **CYNICAL** PERSON WILL ALWAYS <u>SEE</u> A <u>NICKEL</u> -- A DESIRE FOR MONEY -- BEHIND OTHER PEOPLE'S ACTIONS.

- It is rather **cynical** of you to believe that the lifeguard saved that drowning dog only in order to receive a reward.

- Unlike DeMarcus, who is optimistic, upbeat, and sanguine, Luis is **cynical** and uses bitter irony and biting sarcasm to expose in others what he views as selfishness.

Immutable

not changing, not susceptible to change

Think of: **Not mutate able**

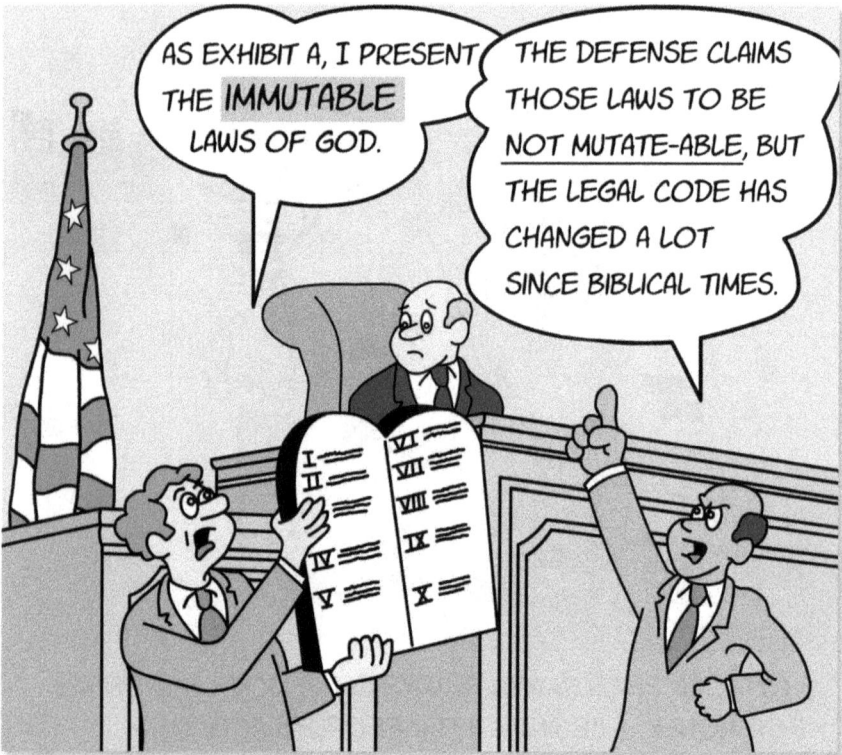

- Many people think of the human species as **immutable**, but scientific evidence has shown that we continue to evolve. For example, over the past 2000 years, the incidence of lactose intolerance has decreased in humans, probably because the ability to tolerate milk has helped people survive periods of drought.

- While the United States constitution is very difficult to amend, it is not meant to be **immutable**.

Unbiased

impartial, fair, just, neutral; having no bias or prejudice; not favoring one side more than another

Think of: **Not buy us**

- A jury must be **unbiased** in reaching a verdict and must decide a case based on facts and not personal preference.

- The two companies are seeking an **unbiased** outside observer who can help them settle their disagreement.

Oblivious

not paying attention, unaware, unmindful, forgetting or overlooking something

Think of: **Overlooking the obvious**

WHEN A FLOOD FILLED THE ROOM, IAN REMAINED *OBLIVIOUS, OVERLOOKING THE OBVIOUS* AND COMPLETING HIS TEST.

- An earthquake shook the room, but Nicole was so engrossed in her book that she remained **oblivious**.

- The senator angered his followers by remaining willfully **oblivious** to their concerns.

Extricate

to remove from difficulty or danger, to release from an unpleasant situation

Think of: **Extract skate**

WHEN KATE DECIDED TO SKATE ON THIN ICE, ONE OF HER SKATES GOT STUCK, AND HER FRIEND HAD TO EXTRICATE HER BY EXTRACTING THE TRAPPED SKATE.

- Three people were successfully **extricated** from the roof of the burning building by helicopter.

- Anthony could not **extricate** himself from trouble when he was caught spray-painting the bathroom.

1. I wouldn't risk setting sail in this storm; your voyage into the approaching hurricane would be extremely ____.
   (A) Indolent **(B)** Perilous **(C)** Cynical **(D)** Unbiased **(E)** Oblivious

2. Your brother is likely to take your side in our argument and would not be a good judge. We need to find someone who is _____.
   (A) Indolent **(B)** Perilous **(C)** Cynical **(D)** Unbiased **(E)** Oblivious

3. The baby kittens cried out for milk; but, strangely, their mother was ____ to their cries and completely ignored them.
   (A) Indolent **(B)** Perilous **(C)** Cynical **(D)** Unbiased **(E)** Oblivious

4. Do not count on a person who is _____ to get a lot of work done.
   (A) Indolent **(B)** Perilous **(C)** Cynical **(D)** Unbiased **(E)** Oblivious

5. I am _____ of your motives; in my mind, you contributed to the cause, not out of a spirit of altruism or benevolence, but out of greed.
   (A) Indolent **(B)** Perilous **(C)** Cynical **(D)** Unbiased **(E)** Oblivious

6. Impasse
   (A) Laziness **(B)** A deadlock or standoff **(C)** An opposing viewpoint
   (D) Neutrality or impartiality **(E)** A break or gap

7. Antithetical
   (A) Diametrically opposed **(B)** Dangerous **(C)** Lazy **(D)** Cheerful and excited
   (E) Unaware or unconcerned

8. Ebullient
   (A) Fair and impartial **(B)** Pessimistic **(C)** Not changeable
   (D) Exactly opposite **(E)** Full of cheerful excitement or enthusiasm

9. Immutable
   (A) Not happy **(B)** Not sleepy **(C)** Not aware **(D)** Not changing
   (E) Not depressed

10. Extricate
    (A) Make worse **(B)** Make better **(C)** Remove from danger
    (D) Doubt someone's motives **(E)** Study carefully

Diatribe

a bitter and abusive verbal attack or criticism

Think of: **Diet Tribe**

YOU'RE DIETING TOO MUCH! LOOK AT YOU! SKINNY AS CARROT STICKS!

THE PILGRIM WENT OFF ON A DIATRIBE AGAINST THE DIET TRIBE BECAUSE THE TRIBE'S EXTREME DIETING CAUSED THEIR BODIES TO SHRINK DANGEROUSLY THIN.

- Spray-painting the bathroom earned Anthony a twenty-minute **diatribe** from Principal Skinner and a suspension from the school.

- One can visit the gritty corner of 16th Street and Mission in San Francisco and often find someone standing on a bench, going off on a **diatribe** about the evils of "the system."

Slovenly

sloppy, untidy, unclean, negligent in appearance, **disheveled**, **unkempt**

Think of: **Sloppy**

JOE IS SUCH A <u>SLOPPY</u> EATER THAT HIS APPEARANCE HAS BECOME SLOVENLY.

- That poor child of negligent parents always seems to have a **slovenly** appearance.

- Oscar's ketchup and guacamole-stained shirt and mud-smeared pants testify to his **slovenly** habits.

Abstemious

eating and drinking in moderation, not indulgent

Think of: **Abby's steam room**

YOU MUST BE ABSTEMIOUS TO ENTER ABBY'S STEAM ROOM, BECAUSE IT IS A PLACE OF QUIET MEDITATION -- NOT A PLACE FOR INDULGENT EATING AND DRINKING.

- The nun lives an **abstemious** lifestyle in her convent, sleeping on a bare mattress in a dormitory and subsisting on two lean meals per day.

- People who tend to overindulge in their consumption of food and drink during the holidays would do well to offset their indulgent behavior with an **abstemious** period of equal duration.

Efficacious

capable of producing a result, having the power to produce a desired effect

Think of: **F cases**

THE BOY HAD AN **EFFICACIOUS** WAY OF HIDING HIS FAILING TEST PAPERS FROM HIS PARENTS. HE HID THEM IN HIS SECRET "F CASES."

- In my family, a shampoo made from olive, rosemary, tea tree, and eucalyptus oils has proven to be an **efficacious** remedy for head lice.

- Naliyah found soaking in the hot springs to be an **efficacious** treatment for the muscle tension in her back.

Insatiable

impossible to satiate or satisfy, always wanting more

Think of: **Not satisfy-able**

- Sharks have an **insatiable** appetite and are constantly in motion, hunting for food.
- Despite the weak global economy, wealthy art buyers worldwide continue to show an **insatiable** appetite for quality contemporary paintings.

Tout

to praise or promote, to publicize or recommend

Think of: **Shout out**

- I **tout** the accomplishments of science and the amazing array of technological devices that science has given the world.

- Since every professional scout **touted** the college quarterback so highly for his talent and character, the young player was selected first in the NFL draft.

Deft

skillful, **adroit**, clever, **dexterous**, nimble; characterized by skill and facility

Think of: **Defeat**

BECAUSE HE HAD AN ADVANTAGE OF HAVING EIGHT ARMS, THE OCTOPUS WAS A DEFT PING-PONG PLAYER, WHO COULD DEFEAT ALL CHALLENGERS.

- The simple-to-use but sturdy leaves of this attractive kitchen table exemplify the **deft** craftsmanship of Dutch Modern carpentry.

- The photographer made **deft** use of the natural light at sunset to bring out the natural beauty of the model and accentuate her ruddy complexion.

Eloquent

having the power of fluent and forceful speech, persuasive and movingly expressive

Think of: **Ella is quoted**

. . . AND THAT WAS A VERY ELOQUENT QUOTE FROM ELLA.

KNKN

BECAUSE SHE IS SO ELOQUENT, ELLA IS QUOTED ON TV ALL THE TIME.

- Ella is quoted on TV all the time because she is so **eloquent**.
- The President's **eloquent** speech on healing the divides of the nation moved people everywhere.

Jettison

to discard or abandon, to throw out or cast overboard

Think of: **Jet is in**

THE PRIVATE JET IS IN SERVICE FOR YOUR TRIP TO NEW YORK.

SWEET !

A GROUP OF FRIENDS *JETTISON* THEIR PLANS FOR A ROAD TRIP WHEN THEY LEARN A PRIVATE JET IS IN SERVICE FOR THEIR PERSONAL USE.

- After her grandparents passed away, Kierra decided that it was finally time to **jettison** the ancient receipts and dusty take-out menus that cluttered their home.

- In order to achieve long-term economic success and a cleaner environment, our country needs to **jettison** its dependence on oil and develop "greener," more sustainable sources of energy.

Stealthy

secretive, cunning, furtive; done quietly and cautiously

Think of: **Steal thy glasses**

" ROBIN HOOD'S GANG IS A *STEALTHY* BUNCH. IF YOU ARE NOT CAUTIOUS THEY WILL STEAL THY GLASSES RIGHT OFF THY FACE. "

- The thief was able to gain entry to the house by **stealthy** means.
- When Al made a **stealthy** attempt to take Jen's SAT exam in her place – in exchange for $2000 – he got caught and was expelled from school.

1. Ann's lifestyle can be described as _____, because she never indulges in luxury.

    (A) Slovenly **(B)** Abstemious **(C)** Efficacious **(D)** Insatiable **(E)** Deft

2. The _____ speaker was able to move and inspire the audience with his words.

    (A) Slovenly **(B)** Efficacious **(C)** Abstemious **(D)** Eloquent **(E)** Stealthy

3. Because we could not convince the boy to share his marbles with us, we made a/an _____ attempt to obtain them by trickery.

    (A) Slovenly **(B)** Stealthy **(C)** Insatiable **(D)** Eloquent **(E)** Efficacious

4. Our new puppy is so _____, we can never keep up with his food needs.

    (A) Efficacious **(B)** Stealthy **(C)** Insatiable **(D)** Deft **(E)** Eloquent

5. Ed advised his friend, "I wouldn't ask the girl out looking like that. Your ____ appearance and dirty clothes are a certain turn-off."

    (A) Slovenly **(B)** Stealthy **(C)** Abstemious **(D)** Deft **(E)** Eloquent

6. The new medicine has proven quite _____ at curing insomnia.

    (A) Insatiable **(B)** Stealthy **(C)** Abstemious **(D)** Efficacious **(E)** Slovenly

7. The leader of that country has been highly praised; his ____ handling of every political crisis has allowed him to move the nation in the right direction.

    (A) Abstemious **(B)** Insatiable **(C)** Stealthy **(D)** Indolent **(E)** Deft

8. Diatribe

    (A) abusive verbal attack **(B)** Friendly remark **(C)** Eating regimen
    (D) A situation from which progress cannot be made
    (E) Arrogance or excessive pride

9. Tout

    (A) Praise **(B)** Criticize **(C)** Discard **(D)** Mislead **(E)** Evacuate

10. Jettison

    (A) Glean or gather **(B)** Embarrass **(C)** Promote or praise
    (D) Remove from danger **(E)** Discard or abandon

Flourish

to **prosper**, **thrive**, or be successful; to grow well or do well;
to be strong and healthy

Think of: **Floor rich**

BECAUSE THEIR FLOORING BUSINESS IS *FLOURISHING*,
FLOORS HAVE MADE THEM RICH.

- Mosquitoes flourish in warm, damp environments.
- I predict that Malik's new business will flourish because he has opened a popular restaurant in an upscale area that severely lacks eating options.

Austere

strict, severe, stern, somber, grave; rigorously self-disciplined; without luxury

Think of: **Austin's tear**

AUSTIN'S TEAR IS EVIDENCE OF THE AUSTERE LIFE HE LEADS IN PRISON.

- Be prepared for an **austere** regimen of hard work if you join the army.
- In that religious sect, the congregation adheres to an **austere** life and refrains from any luxury or indulgence.

Prognosticate

to predict or foretell future events

Think of: **Pro knows tick rate**

BE CAREFUL. I PREDICT THAT EXACTLY FOUR OF YOU WILL RECEIVE TICK BITES THIS WEEKEND.

HOW CAN HE POSSIBLY KNOW THAT ?

THE <u>PRO</u> SCOUT <u>KNOWS</u> THE <u>TICK RATE</u> SO IS ABLE TO PROGNOSTICATE THE NUMBER OF TICK BITES.

- Calvin has a certain knack for being able to **prognosticate** the outcome of football games.

- A financial analyst who can accurately **prognosticate** trends in the stock market will be very successful.

Ostentatious

characterized by a vulgar display of wealth; given to conspicuous, pretentious, and extravagant show in an attempt to impress others

Think of: **Austin's tent spacious**

HE MAKES SUCH AN OSTENTATIOUS DISPLAY OF HIS WEALTH THAT EVEN AUSTEN'S TENT IS MORE SPACIOUS THAN MOST PEOPLE'S HOMES.

- Austin flaunts his wealth even when "roughing it" in nature: even his tent and camping gear are **ostentatious**.

- When the celebrity attended the event wearing one million dollars worth of diamonds, observers criticized the **ostentatious** display of wealth.

Coerce

to compel by force, intimidation, or authority; to make somebody do something against his or her will by using force or threats

Think of: **Cop force**

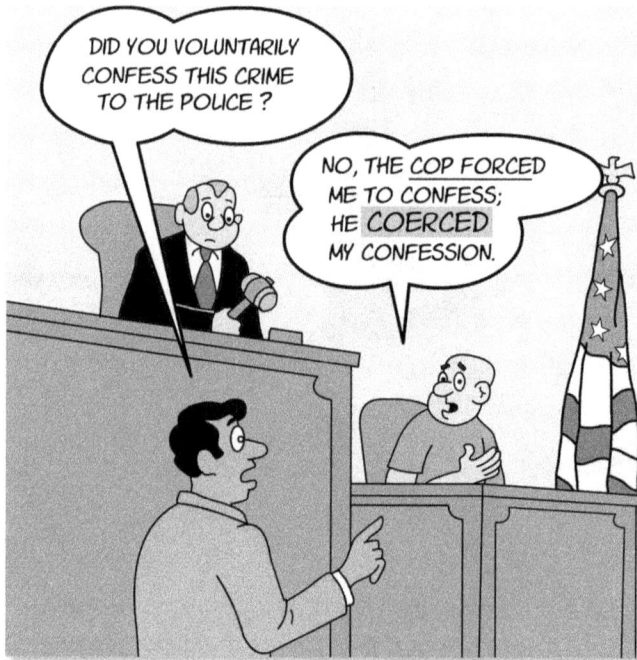

- I did not voluntarily admit to the crime; the police **coerced** my confession. Because it was illegal for the cop to use force to **coerce** me, I was later acquitted. (Note: to acquit = declare not guilty, free from a charge or blame.)

- By using its monopoly on the market and dominating position in the economy, the large company was able to **coerce** its smaller competitors into take-over agreements.

Elucidate

to make clear, to clarify, to make comprehensible

Think of: **Eel Lucy ate**

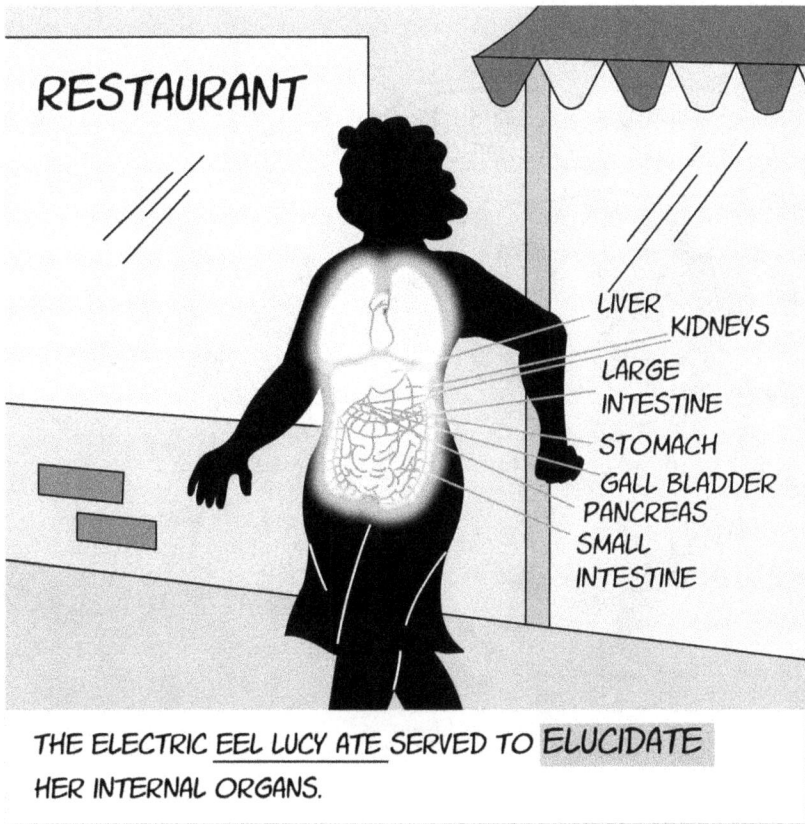

RESTAURANT

LIVER
KIDNEYS
LARGE INTESTINE
STOMACH
GALL BLADDER
PANCREAS
SMALL INTESTINE

THE ELECTRIC EEL LUCY ATE SERVED TO ELUCIDATE HER INTERNAL ORGANS.

- The teacher liked much of the essay but thought that the student needed to **elucidate** her thesis more clearly.

- As he projected his slide-show presentation onto the screen, Gordon explained to the class, "These charts and graphs should **elucidate** my point."

Supercilious

arrogant, contemptuous, **haughty**, disdainful

Think of: **Super is all of us**

- Hannah shouted at her soccer opponents, "Compared to your sucky team, super is all of us," an arrogant and grammatically-flawed remark which caused others to label her **supercilious**.

- The United States has been accused of having a **supercilious** attitude toward the rest of the world, but perhaps the planet's global powers always face such accusations.

Circumspect

prudent, cautious, watchful

Think of: **Circle inspect**

WHEN THE POLICEMAN ENTERED THE GANGSTER'S DEN, HE TOOK A CIRCUMSPECT APPROACH, MAKING A FULL CIRCLE INSPECTION FOR DANGER.

- The police officer took a **circumspect** approach when entering the gangsters' den.

- In the future, I will be **circumspect** about taking the girl at her word, since I have caught her in several untruths.

Prosaic

commonplace or dull, straightforward and unimaginative

Think of: **Prose**

COMPARED TO POETRY, A CREATIVE AND IMAGINATIVE WRITING FORM, PROSE IS RATHER PROSAIC.

- Compared to the vivid poetry of Edgar Allen Poe, the writing in an instruction manual is rather **prosaic**.

- The politician's suggestion that the energy crisis can be solved by turning off more lights seems to be a rather **prosaic**, even simplistic, response to a complex issue.

Lucrative

profitable

Think of: **Lou creative**

BECAUSE <u>LOU</u> IS SO <u>CREATIVE</u>, HIS BUSINESS IS <u>LUCRATIVE</u>.

- The power of the internet to reach a global audience has enabled companies such as Facebook and Google to rank among the most **lucrative** businesses of all time.

- While the actor's love is to perform stage plays in front of live audiences, he must take many jobs in television ads because they are far more **lucrative**.

1. No amount of force will _____ me into confessing to a crime that I didn't commit.

   (A) Flourish **(B)** Prognosticate **(C)** Coerce **(D)** Elucidate **(E)** Circumspect

2. The woman claimed she was a prophet and that she could accurately _____ future events.

   (A) Flourish **(B)** Prognosticate **(C)** Coerce **(D)** Elucidate **(E)** Circumspect

3. In this essay, your main point seemed somewhat ambiguous. Can you _____ the thesis and explain your ideas more clearly?

   (A) Flourish **(B)** Prognosticate **(C)** Coerce **(D)** Elucidate **(E)** Circumspect

4. Snails have been able to _____ in my garden without any predators, and so they have become extremely abundant.

   (A) Flourish **(B)** Prognosticate **(C)** Coerce **(D)** Elucidate **(E)** Circumspect

5. Due to the financial crisis, the company has adopted a/an _____ program, which includes reducing all luxuries and expenses.

   (A) Austere **(B)** Ostentatious **(C)** Supercilious **(D)** Prosaic **(E)** Lucrative

6. Tony is now a millionaire thanks to his _____ construction business.

   (A) Austere **(B)** Ostentatious **(C)** Supercilious **(D)** Prosaic **(E)** Lucrative

7. The celebrity's mansion reflects his lavish tastes and is seen as a/an _____ display of his wealth.

   (A) Austere **(B)** Ostentatious **(C)** Supercilious **(D)** Circumspect **(E)** Lucrative

8. We must take a/an _____ approach to the crisis because any wrong decision could have disastrous consequences. Let's deliberate carefully before taking action.

   (A) Prosaic **(B)** Ostentatious **(C)** Supercilious **(D)** Circumspect **(E)** Lucrative

9. The writer believed her new book to be ground-breaking and innovative, but I found the content rather _____.

   (A) Prosaic **(B)** Ostentatious **(C)** Supercilious **(D)** Circumspect **(E)** Austere

10. John's arrogant comments and boastful remarks reflect his _____ nature.

    (A) Prosaic **(B)** Lucrative **(C)** Supercilious **(D)** Circumspect **(E)** Austere

Idiosyncrasy

a characteristic, habit, or mannerism that is peculiar to an individual; a way of behaving or thinking peculiar to an individual or group

Think of: **I do sinks like crazy**

JUAN'S PARTICULAR IDIOSYNCRASY IS SCRUBBING DOWN ALL THE SINKS UPON FIRST ENTERING A PERSON'S HOME.

- Juan's particular **idiosyncrasy** is to scrub the sinks of his home frequently in order to prevent bacteria buildup.

- The reclusive writer told me that I would have to adjust to the **idiosyncrasies** of life in the desert.

Panacea

a cure-all, a remedy for all diseases or problems

Think of: **Panic see ya'**

- While there are a variety of somewhat effective options for treating cancer, there is no **panacea**.

- There is no **panacea** for the problems facing the planet; only by hard work and dedicated effort will we begin to make progress.

Provocation

an act that incites anger, provokes irritation, or causes indignation

Think of: **Pro vacation**

WHEN TINA BECAME A <u>PRO</u> AT TAKING <u>VACATION</u> TIME, HER OFFICE MATES CONSIDERED THE ACT A **PROVOCATION**.

- When the militant nation amassed its armies at the border, the country's neighbor took the act as a **provocation**.

- The employer's threat to drastically cut workers' salaries and vacation time was considered a **provocation**.

Ameliorate

to make better or improve

Think of: **"A-meal you rate?"**

- The new management has **ameliorated** working conditions at the restaurant, which in turn has ameliorated employee morale.

- Our business will flourish if we **ameliorate** the quality of our services.

Pinnacle

1. high point, **zenith** 2. a lofty peak or a tall, pointed formation, such as a turret or spire at the top of a roof

Think of: **Pin ankle**

WHEN BUTCH WAS AT THE PINNACLE OF HIS WRESTLING CAREER, HE COULD PIN AN OPPONENT JUST WITH HIS ANKLE.

- At the **pinnacle** of his basketball career, Michael Jordan was able to carry the Chicago Bulls to six championship rings.

- The United States was at the **pinnacle** of its economic power after World War II, when the country accounted for about one-quarter of all goods produced worldwide.

Cogent

forcefully convincing and compelling, well-argued

Think of: **Convincing gent**

MARCUS IS A <u>CONVINCING GENT</u>, BECAUSE HIS PRESENTATIONS ARE SO **COGENT**.

- The class was fascinated and stimulated by the professor's **cogent** presentation.

- Idealab founder Bill Gross makes a **cogent** argument in favor of solar energy in a video frequently watched on YouTube.

Lackadaisical

without interest or effort, without energy or enthusiasm, **lethargic**

Think of: **Lacking daisies**

WHILE ALL THE OTHER PERFORMERS WERE ELATED AT RECEIVING BOUQUETS OF DAISIES AFTER THE PLAY, MAYA FELT LACKADAISICAL BECAUSE SHE WAS THE ONLY ONE LACKING DAISIES.

- The bereft widow felt **lackadaisical** after the loss of her husband. (Note: *bereft* = lacking, deprived, suffering a loss.)

- The football coach demanded every player's full determination and would not tolerate **lackadaisical** effort.

Debilitate

to weaken, **enervate**, enfeeble, or incapacitate; to sap the strength and energy of someone or something

Think of: **Ability**

- The auto accident nearly killed the woman and left her **debilitated** for months after the collision.
- Recurrent knee injuries **debilitated** Greg Oden, the Ohio State basketball star, and severely shortened his professional career.

Enervate

to weaken or destroy the strength, force, or vitality of someone

Think of: **Energy ate**

THE TUG-OF-WAR CONTEST COMPLETELY ATE ALEX'S ENERGY, AND NOW HE FEELS ENERVATED.

- When the tourist traveled through Tamil Nadu in southern India during the hot season of April, she felt **enervated** by the constant sun.

- The woman's habit of running around between appointments without even stopping to take a break for lunch left her completely **enervated** by the end of the day.

Fabrication

an invented statement or account devised to deceive; a deliberately false or improbable statement

Think of: **Fib creation**

TOO MUCH <u>FIB CREATION</u> MADE HIS STATEMENT TO THE POLICE A TOTAL **FABRICATION.**

- The police believed the man's story to be a total **fabrication** because many of his assertions contradicted known facts.

- The woman's tax returns are a complete **fabrication** and a poorly-disguised attempt to avoid paying taxes.

Review #19

1. When facts revealed that one part of the suspect's story was a lie, the police began to believe his entire account of the events to be a/an _____.
    (A) Idiosyncrasy **(B)** Panacea **(C)** Provocation **(D)** Pinnacle **(E)** Fabrication

2. To dip the meat in two different curry sauces is the _____ of this particular type of Indian cuisine, specific to one small region of the north.
    (A) Idiosyncrasy **(B)** Panacea **(C)** Provocation **(D)** Pinnacle **(E)** Fabrication

3. Ibuprofen can mitigate the pain of a headache, but it is not a _____; people who suffer from chronic headaches rarely find an ideal remedy but rely upon a variety of treatments, each of which provides some relief.
    (A) Idiosyncrasy **(B)** Panacea **(C)** Provocation **(D)** Pinnacle **(E)** Fabrication

4. At the _____ of his career as a salesman, Bob was selling more than 20 cars per month.
    (A) Idiosyncrasy **(B)** Panacea **(C)** Provocation **(D)** Pinnacle **(E)** Fabrication

5. To flaunt your wealth in front of those poor and hungry children is quite a _____.
    (A) Idiosyncrasy **(B)** Panacea **(C)** Provocation **(D)** Pinnacle **(E)** Fabrication

6. The plan to create new parks, playgrounds, and bike lanes will _____ the quality of life in that town.
    (A) Ameliorate **(B)** Coerce **(C)** Debilitate **(D)** Elucidate **(E)** Enervate

7. The accumulation of injuries will _____ the accident victim for months.
    (A) Ameliorate **(B)** Coerce **(C)** Debilitate **(D)** Prognosticate **(E)** Flourish

8. Cogent
    (A) Listless, lacking energy **(B)** Strict or severe **(C)** Showy, lavish
    (D) Commonplace, ordinary **(E)** Forcefully convincing

9. Lackadaisical
    (A) Stern, somber, grave **(B)** Without interest or effort
    (C) Characterized by a vulgar display of wealth **(D)** Arrogant, contemptuous
    (E) Prudent, cautious, watchful

10. Enervate
    (A) To explain one's cause **(B)** To prosper or thrive **(C)** To predict or foretell
    (D) To sap someone's strength **(E)** To force or compel

Jubilant

expressing great joy or delight

Think of: **Joy be lent**

SINCE YOUR TEAM IS TWO PLAYERS SHORT, WE CAN LOAN YOU JOY FOR THIS GAME.

YAY!

HOORAY!

THE TEAM WAS JUBILANT ABOUT THEIR OPPONENT'S DECISION TO ALLOW JOY TO BE LENT TO THEM FOR THIS GAME.

- The mood on the campus of Columbia University after the football team snapped its historic 44-game losing streak was so **jubilant** that people poured forth from the dorms and closed down Broadway to partake in the spontaneous jubilation.

- Zoe felt **jubilant** after hearing that she was offered her dream job.

Zealot

a person who shows zeal, fervor, or enthusiasm; an enthusiastic supporter of a cause; a fanatically committed person

Think of: **Z a lot**

MARIAH IS INTO MUSICIAN JAY Z A LOT; IN FACT, SHE WORSHIPS HIM SO FANATICALLY THAT PEOPLE CALL HER A ZEALOT.

- It takes a true football **zealot** to go shirtless at the game in sub-zero temperatures, wearing nothing but one letter of his team's name painted on his chest.

- While the addition of bike lanes has been a dramatic improvement to the city, many critics accuse the mayor of being an anti-car **zealot** because he quadrupled parking fees downtown and closed off 18 streets to vehicles.

Callous

showing no concern that other people might be hurt or upset; insensitive, unsympathetic, **indifferent**, hardhearted

Think of: **Call us**

THE PLUMBERS WERE *CALLOUS* TO THE HOMEOWNER'S PROBLEM, SAYING *"CALL US TOMORROW."*

- I found the affluent business leader to be rather **callous** when he turned a deaf ear to the suffering children.
- The woman's hostile attitude demonstrates a **callous** indifference, even to members of her own family.

Rash

acting hastily or without consideration, **impetuous**, thoughtless, reckless

Think of: **Rushed**

WHEN TOBY MADE A <u>RUSHED</u> DECISION TO BUY THE HOUSE TWO SECONDS AFTER ENTERING THE ROOM, HANNAH THOUGHT HE WAS MAKING A RASH DECISION.

- The family made a rather **rash** decision to buy the house five minutes after walking through the front door.

- Joel was **rash** in his decision to attend Brown University based on the school's colors without considering other aspects of the college or waiting to hear where else he'd been admitted.

Impetuous

acting without considering the consequences, done impulsively, **rash**

Think of: **I.M. pet** (an I.M. is an instant message)

CHARLIE MADE AN IMPETUOUS DECISION TO I.M. HIS PET, NOT THINKING ABOUT THE TEXTING CHARGES, OR THE FACT THAT THE DOG COULDN'T READ.

- The man made the **impetuous** decision to let a new friend he met online invest all of his money in a start-up company.

- While Laura makes most of life's important decisions in a thoughtful, rational, and deliberate way, she can be quite **impetuous** when choosing a boyfriend.

Debunk

to prove something wrong or show something to be false

Think of: **D-bunk**

JOE DEBUNKED THE MYTH THAT THE LOCAL FURNITURE FACTORY ONLY MADE GRADE D BUNK BEDS. HE RATES HIS BUNK A+ FOR PERFORMANCE AND QUALITY.

- Joe **debunked** the myth that his local furniture outlet could only make grade D bunk beds when he published a report demonstrating the outstanding performance and quality of such beds.

- Scientists have long since **debunked** the myth that the earth is only 7,000 years old. In fact, the planet formed about 4.5 billion years ago.

Adversity

hardships, difficulties, unfavorable circumstances; a condition of distress or misfortune

Think of: **Ad for city**

" THAT <u>AD FOR</u> THE <u>CITY</u> DEPICTS ONLY THE GLAMOROUS ASPECTS OF URBAN CULTURE AND SHOWS NONE OF THE ADVERSITY. "

- The cast members of the play had to overcome the **adversity** of losing their lead actor just days before opening night.

- Despite years of **adversity** and poverty, the writer ultimately achieved a measure of success and became highly regarded in her field.

Lavish

abundant, generous, extravagant, **profuse**, excessive

Think of: **Leave fish**

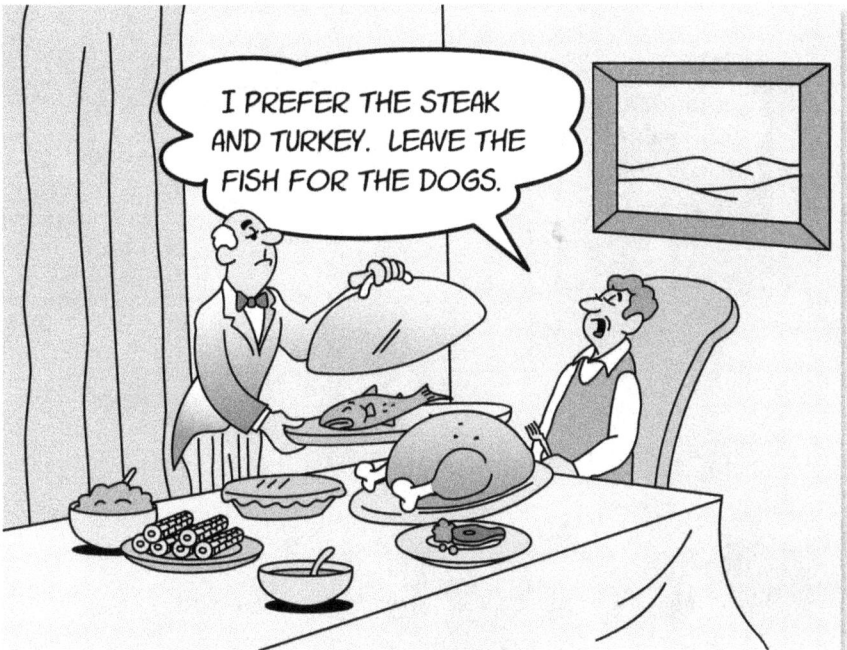

I PREFER THE STEAK AND TURKEY. LEAVE THE FISH FOR THE DOGS.

THE FEAST WAS SO LAVISH, THE CELEBRITY WAS ABLE TO LEAVE THE FISH FOR THE DOGS.

- The celebrity served such a lavish feast in her opulent mansion that, when all the guests were totally sated, enough food was left over for her to declare, "Leave the fish for the dogs."

- The teacher heaped lavish praise upon her students for their outstanding research projects.

Sagacious

wise, **judicious**, **astute**; showing sound judgment or profound knowledge

Think of: **So gracious**

- The student was **sagacious** in studying her vocabulary lists over the weekend because her teacher surprised the class with a test on Monday morning.

- The athlete made the **sagacious** decision to stay in college and complete his education because he knew that football success might prove ephemeral and that a college degree might be useful in the future.

Pervasive

spread throughout, all-encompassing

Think of: **Pour vase sieve**

- Tragically, gang violence has become **pervasive** in many parts of Mexico.

- When I lived in that country, government corruption was so **pervasive** that I had to pay a kind of bribe to obtain any license or important document.

1. In that country, no progress will be made unless the government can end the _____ corruption and violence.

   (A) Jubilant **(B)** Callous **(C)** Rash **(D)** Impetuous **(E)** Pervasive

2. Joe made a _____ decision to attend College X without waiting to hear where else he had been accepted and based his decision solely on the arbitrary flip of a coin.

   (A) Jubilant **(B)** Callous **(C)** Rash **(D)** Lavish **(E)** Sagacious

3. To deny your own mother's request for a ride to the airport seems rather _____.

   (A) Lavish **(B)** Callous **(C)** Sagacious **(D)** Impetuous **(E)** Pervasive

4. Your decision to bring your passport with you proved _____ when the police stopped you and asked for identification.

   (A) Jubilant **(B)** Rash **(C)** Sagacious **(D)** Impetuous **(E)** Pervasive

5. At the celebrity's mansion, the feast was so _____ that there were gourmet dishes of fish left over for the dogs.

   (A) Lavish **(B)** Rash **(C)** Callous **(D)** Impetuous **(E)** Pervasive

6. At the gala wedding celebration, the happy couple was in a _____ mood.

   (A) Lavish **(B)** Rash **(C)** Callous **(D)** Jubilant **(E)** Sagacious

7. On a sudden _____ whim, Joey led us on a train to the middle of nowhere.

   (A) Lavish **(B)** Impetuous **(C)** Pervasive **(D)** Jubilant **(E)** Sagacious

8. Zealot

   (A) Hardships or difficulties **(B)** Peculiarity **(C)** Cure-all **(D)** High point zenith **(E)** A person who shows fervor, or enthusiasm

9. Debunk

   (A) Verify or ascertain **(B)** Improve or make better **(C)** Weaken or destroy **(D)** Caution or forbid **(E)** Prove false

10. Adversity

    (A) An act that incites anger or provokes irritation **(B)** A fanatically committed person **(C)** Unfavorable circumstances **(D)** An invented statement **(E)** A lofty peak or tall, pointed formation

Spurious

not authentic, not genuine, not valid, counterfeit

Think of: **Furious**

DAD WAS <u>FURIOUS</u> WHEN HE LEARNED THAT HE'D PAID $5000 FOR A COUNTERFEIT DIAMOND, A **SPURIOUS** IMITATION.

- Dad called the diamond a fake and the ring a **spurious** imitation.
- The company's **spurious** accounting and deceitful tax returns have triggered an FBI investigation.

Spurn

to reject contemptuously

Think of: **Spurs**

JUAN SPURNS USING SPURS, WHICH HURT THE HORSE, AND
COAXES HIS STEED WITH GENTLE WHISPERS.

- I invited Rose to the prom, but she **spurned** my invitation.
- The government of that belligerent country has **spurned** all peace overtures.

Caustic

1. critical, bitter, biting, sarcastic 2. capable of burning or corroding

Think of: **Cause stinks**

WHEN LAURA ASKED ED TO SUPPORT THE CAUSE, HE MADE THE *CAUSTIC* COMMENT, "YOUR CAUSE STINKS ! "

- When asked to help save the frogs, Ed made the **caustic** comment, "Your cause stinks."

- Hydrochloric acid is a highly **caustic** substance and should not be touched with bare skin.

Subjective

pertaining to a particular individual, placing emphasis on one's own opinions

Think of: **Subject I've**

- The potential juror in the case was dismissed when she admitted that her decision might be **subjective** because she knew the victim.

- The percentage of people considered to have successfully passed this test is somewhat **subjective**, because the definition of success was never clearly defined.

Intrepid

fearless, bold, daring, courageous

Think of: **Inch rapid**

THE <u>INCH</u> WORM IS PERHAPS TOO INTREPID, EVEN
FOOLHARDY, IN ITS <u>RAPID</u> DASH.

- The intrepid firefighters bravely entered the burning building in a desperate attempt to rescue the people trapped inside.

- The intrepid soldier charged the enemy position without regard for his own life.

Stringent

strict, severe, restrictive, binding

Think of: **Strict aunt**

Rules
Bedtime...... 8 pm
Showers .... 2 Min.
No music in room
No pets
Vacuum daily

MAYA HATED STAYING WITH HER STRICT AUNT, BECAUSE THE RULES WERE SO STRINGENT.

- The **stringent** rules at the boarding school frustrate the children and allow little leeway for having fun.

- The **stringent** graduation requirements at that college make it exceedingly difficult for students to graduate.

Obtrusive

1. protruding, sticking out 2. self-assertive, brash

Think of: **Obvious**

" POOR AMY, THAT PIMPLE ON HER NOSE IS SO *OBTRUSIVE*, IT IS OBVIOUS TO EVERYONE FROM A MILE AWAY. "

- Many people dislike the crowds and **obtrusive** noise associated with life in a big city.

- The oversized wristwatch is useful for telling time, but I find its appearance to be rather **obtrusive**.

Eccentric

deviating from convention or custom, peculiar, odd

Think of: **Ex-center Rick**

EX-CENTER RICK IS SO ECCENTRIC THAT IN REGULAR DAILY LIFE, HE IMAGINES HE'S STILL ON THE BASKETBALL COURT.

- A man who routinely blocks his co-workers' attempts to throw out trash and who considers life at the office to be an ongoing basketball game may be called "**eccentric**."

- The author Oscar Wilde was considered **eccentric** because he wore flamboyant clothes, decorated his room with peacock feathers, and wandered the streets of Oxford with a pet lobster on a leash.

Stoic

one who appears unmoved and unaffected by grief, joy, pleasure, or pain

Think of: **Stow it**

- Despite the death of his friend, Ed remained **stoic** and did not even cry or flinch at the funeral.
- The **stoic** remained stony-faced and did not show any emotion.

Duplicity

deception, deceit, double-dealing, fraud, trickery

Think of: **Duplicate city**

"I HAVE TO MAKE SURE IT'S NOT COUNTERFEIT OR DUPLICATE. IN DUPLICATE CITY, THERE IS MUCH DUPLICITY."

- A city where money is duplicated and circulated illegally will become known for **duplicity**.

- The company's financial **duplicity** included hiding 500 million dollars in losses while reporting a profit.

Review #21

1. The teacher's _____ comment about Jim's research project made him feel dejected about the hard work he had done.
    (A) Eccentric (B) Caustic (C) Obtrusive (D) Intrepid (E) Stringent

2. The coach made a rather _____ decision to base the starting team on points scored alone without consideration of defense or assists.
    (A) Obtrusive (B) Caustic (C) Subjective (D) Spurious (E) Stringent

3. The _____ writer was known to sleep in the attic while allowing his pets to inhabit the main floor.
    (A) Subjective (B) Eccentric (C) Intrepid (D) Spurious (E) Stringent

4. It would be tragic to convict an innocent person based on _____ evidence.
    (A) Obtrusive (B) Eccentric (C) Intrepid (D) Spurious (E) Caustic

5. A relaxed environment at a university is more conducive to learning than a system of _____ rules and severe punishments.
    (A) Obtrusive (B) Caustic (C) Intrepid (D) Spurious (E) Stringent

6. Who will be _____ enough to join me on the midnight hike to the top of the volcano?
    (A) Intrepid (B) Caustic (C) Spurious (D) Subjective (E) Stringent

7. Kelly found her house guest to be rather _____; he did nothing to make himself small and, in fact, did everything to occupy her living room.
    (A) Intrepid (B) Eccentric (C) Intrepid (D) Subjective (E) Obtrusive

8. Spurn
    (A) Inhabit (B) Reject (C) Prove false (D) Weaken (E) Defeat

9. Stoic
    (A) A person free of hate (B) A person immune to disease
    (C) A person unmoved by emotion (D) A storage system (E) A mine or quarry

10. Duplicity
    (A) Enthusiastic encouragement (B) Person unaffected by grief
    (C) Deceit or trickery (D) Hardships or difficulties
    (E) An enthusiastic supporter of a cause

Exemplary

worthy of imitation, serving as a good model or example

Think of: **Example**

HER BEHAVIOR IN CLASS HAS BEEN EXEMPLARY – SHE MAKES A GOOD EXAMPLE FOR ALL THE OTHER STUDENTS.

- The teacher made sure to praise the student's **exemplary** behavior in class.

- Most employees within that company seek to emulate their director's **exemplary** actions and respect for others.

Fallacious

containing a mistake or false notion, **erroneous**, illogical

Think of: **False aces**

IT IS FALLACIOUS TO THINK THAT CHRIS WILL WIN THIS POKER HAND. HE IS HOLDING FALSE ACES, FROM A DIFFERENT DECK.

- The **fallacious** idea that the sun revolves around the earth held sway in many quarters for centuries.

- The conjecture that the earth is shaped like a flat disk has been proven **fallacious**.

Defer

to yield or submit to the opinions or judgment of another

Think of: **Deaf ear**

CHARLES DECIDED TO DEFER TO HIS FRIEND'S WISHES WHEN HIS FRIEND TURNED A DEAF EAR TO HIS IDEA.

- Since you are the authority in this subject, I will **defer** to your opinion.
- The hikers **deferred** to the park ranger's wisdom in choosing their camp site.

Castigate

criticize, reprimand, **rebuke**, **chastise**, **malign**

Think of: **Cast gate**

THE DIRECTOR CASTIGATES THE ACTORS FOR HAVING A CAST ONLY GATE.

- The student was **castigated** for pulling the fire alarm as a joke.
- Thoughtful people everywhere will **castigate** a dictator who holds power by force and suppresses human rights.

Steadfast

firm in purpose; fixed, loyal, constant, unwavering, unswerving

Think of: **Steady fast**

- The woman's **steadfast** love for and commitment to her children led her to take a second job in order to finance their education.

- The man's **steadfast** refusal to pay the rent is due to his landlord's failure to provide basic maintenance and safety requirements in the apartment.

Acquiesce

agree passively, submit or comply without protest

Think of: **A queasy yes**

BEN RELUCTANTLY **ACQUIESCED** TO CLEAN THE BOYS'
BATHROOM WITH A QUEASY YES.

- Ben didn't really want to clean the bathroom but **acquiesced** because he felt compelled to do his share.

- The child hated to do his chores but **acquiesced** to his Dad's request in the hope of earning ice cream.

Acumen

keen insight or judgment

Think of: **Accurate men**

THE <u>ACCURATE MEN</u> WHO CORRECTLY PREDICT TRENDS IN THE STOCK MARKET DEMONSTRATE FINANCIAL **ACUMEN**.

- The professor is highly regarded for his **acumen** in analyzing economic trends.

- The teacher asked his class, "Who can demonstrate his or her physics **acumen** by explaining why the heavy stone and light stone, when dropped together, hit the ground at the same time?"

Astute

perceptive, **shrewd**, wise, **sagacious**, having insight or acumen

Think of: **An A student**

THE A STUDENT IS VERY **ASTUTE**.

- The tutor's **astute** observation helped the student solve a challenging problem.

- The country's Prime Minister exhibited **astute** leadership in her handling of the complex diplomatic skirmish.

Enmity

hostility, hatred, ill will

Think of: **'N mighty**

A PERSON WHO THINKS HE'S HIGH A_N_D M_IGHTY_ WILL
EARN THE ENMITY OF HIS PEERS.

- The child's tendency to shout out in class earned him the **enmity** of his peers.

- When the military ruler imposed religious law upon the country, he received the **enmity** of secular citizens throughout the nation.

Thrifty

wisely economical, **frugal**, managing money or resources in a cautious and sensible way

Think of: **Three-fifty**

- My mother is such a **thrifty** shopper, she can always find new shoes or an elegant dress for $3.50.

- The new financial manager's **thrifty** use of company funds has turned the business around and helped the company turn a loss into a profit.

1. The retired woman was able to survive on a meager income only because she was so ___ with her money and never indulged recklessly.
    (A) Exemplary **(B)** Fallacious **(C)** Steadfast **(D)** Astute **(E)** Thrifty

2. Her years of volunteer work helping kids in school learn to read is evidence of a _____ lifetime commitment to education.
    (A) Exemplary **(B)** Fallacious **(C)** Steadfast **(D)** Astute **(E)** Thrifty

3. One incorrect and _____ idea that fueled European colonization of Africa and perpetuated slavery was the notion that Africans were somehow genetically inferior and in need of white man's help.
    (A) Exemplary **(B)** Fallacious **(C)** Steadfast **(D)** Astute **(E)** Thrifty

4. Through her _____ behavior both in and out of the classroom, the student has become an excellent role-model for her peers.
    (A) Exemplary **(B)** Fallacious **(C)** Steadfast **(D)** Astute **(E)** Thrifty

5. Ed made the _____ observation that we had everything ready for our journey to the Black Rock Desert, except the most important part: water.
    (A) Exemplary **(B)** Fallacious **(C)** Steadfast **(D)** Astute **(E)** Thrifty

6. The dad severely _____ his child for playing with the cigarette lighter and setting the house on fire.
    (A) Deferred **(B)** Castigated **(C)** Acquiesced **(D)** Debunked **(E)** Enervated

7. We always do things your way; just this once can you _____ to my wishes?
    (A) Defer **(B)** Castigate **(C)** Ameliorate **(D)** Debunk **(E)** Spurn

8. I didn't really want to clean the bathrooms, but I had to _____ to the drill sergeant's order.
    (A) Mitigate **(B)** Castigate **(C)** Acquiesce **(D)** Debunk **(E)** Spurn

9. Acumen
    (A) An act that incites anger **(B)** High point **(C)** Deception, fraud, trickery
    (D) Hatred, hostility **(E)** Keen insight

10. Enmity
    (A) Zenith **(B)** A bitter and abusive verbal attack **(C)** Adversary
    (D) Hostility, hatred, ill will **(E)** Good judgment

Surmount

overcome, conquer, prevail over, mount, climb to the top of

Think of: **Sir, mount**

- If you expect me to mount that horse, I will first need to **surmount** my fear of horses.

- In many countries, minority groups have had to **surmount** challenging obstacles in order to achieve success and acceptance within society.

Magnanimous

generous, kind, **philanthropic**, **benevolent**, **munificent**

Think of: **Magnet 'n' mouse**

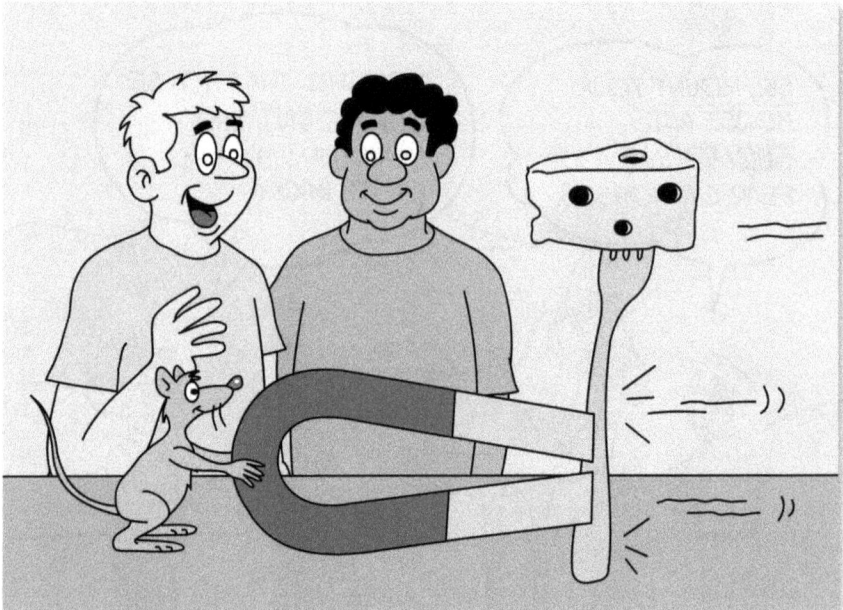

" *OUR* **MAGNANIMOUS** *UNCLE GIVES US GENEROUS GIFTS LIKE THIS MAGNET 'N A TRAINED MOUSE.* "

- The **magnanimous** benefactor gave $10 million to charity.
- The woman has been **magnanimous** with her time and money; and as a result of her dedicated efforts, hundreds of lives have been saved.

Mollify

to calm or soothe someone who is angry or upset; **pacify**, **placate**, **appease**

Think of: **Molly fries**

" MOLLY GETS UPSET WHENEVER WE FEED HER FRESH AND HEALTHY VEGETABLES. WE CAN ONLY MOLLIFY HER BY GIVING MOLLY FRIES. "

- When the teacher showed up to work drunk, the principal could only **mollify** enraged parents by promising to dismiss the man from his teaching post.

- The energy company has agreed to install high-tech filters on the smokestacks of its coal-burning power plant in order to **mollify** concerns about pollution and air quality.

Cantankerous

disagreeable, quarrelsome, ill-tempered, argumentative, **contentious**, peevish

Think of: **Can't anger us**

" *YOU CAN'T ANGER US. WE'RE ALREADY SO GROUCHY AND IRRITABLE. WE'RE CANTANKEROUS.* "

- The comedian Lewis Black adopts a **cantankerous** personality for comic effect and is very funny as a bitter, grumpy man.

- Although the elderly man was mellow and relaxed in his youth, he has become quite **cantankerous** in his old age.

Aloof

at a distance, apart, remote, reserved

Think of: **Alone on the roof**

- Because she never comes down to join the party and sits alone up on the roof, Hannah is seen as **aloof**.

- The British aristocracy is often depicted in fiction as an **aloof** group of idiosyncratic snobs who would be abashed to socialize with mere commoners.

Apprehensive

anxious, uneasy, nervous, fearful

Think of: **Apprehended**

WHEN JOE WAS <u>APPREHENDED</u> BY THE POLICE, HE FELT **APPREHENSIVE**.

- Having to speak in front of a large audience makes many people **apprehensive**.
- Zoe felt **apprehensive** when the police called to inform her that her home had been broken into.

Objective

1. not influenced by personal feelings, unbiased, impartial
2. a goal

Think of: **Object of**

" THE <u>OBJECT OF</u> THIS CLASS IS TO TEACH YOU OBJECTIVE NEWS REPORTING. "

- That is your opinion on the matter, not **objective** fact.
- The jury was able to judge the evidence in a fair and **objective** way.

Mercenary

motivated by money, acting for material reward, influenced by greed

Think of: **More scenery**

BUY OUR GREAT NEW PRODUCT

THE THING-A-MA-WHATCHA-MA-CALLIT

Only $8.99

PLUS $99.00 SHIPPING AND HANDLING

" WE WOULD ENJOY <u>MORE SCENERY</u> IF IT WERE NOT FOR THE MERCENARY METHODS OF THAT COMPANY. "

- Murray doesn't really care for the cause; his motives are **mercenary**, and he stands to score a bundle of money if the project succeeds.

- Some have accused that bank of **mercenary** behavior when it foreclosed on so many people's houses for minor financial delinquencies. (Note: *delinquencies* = failures to fulfill a duty or commitment.)

Catastrophic

disastrous, ruinous, awful, causing damage

Think of: **Cat as trophy**

WHEN HUNTERS USE THE BIG CAT AS A TROPHY, THEIR ACTIONS HAVE A CATASTROPHIC EFFECT ON THE POPULATION OF THE TIGERS WORLDWIDE.

- The combination of climate change, predation, and loss of natural habitat has had a **catastrophic** effect on many species.

- When the big chain store opened a thriving new location downtown, the consequences were **catastrophic** for small, family-owned boutiques in the area.

Vacillate

to waver, sway, **oscillate**, or swing indecisively from one course of action to another

Think of: **Vaccine late**

ELLA TOOK HER FLU VACCINE TOO LATE BECAUSE SHE KEPT VACILLATING ON WHETHER SHE REALLY NEEDED IT.

- The principal could not commit to hiring one of the applicants as the new teacher; in fact, her position seemed to **vacillate** publically from day to day.

- When the judge threatened to reverse his earlier ruling, many accused him of **vacillating**.

Review #23

1. Bob felt ____ about his upcoming job interview and couldn't sleep all night.
   (A) Magnanimous **(B)** Cantankerous **(C)** Aloof **(D)** Apprehensive
   (E) Objective

2. The celebrity came across as rather ____ when she chose to stand alone in the corner rather than having to socialize with non-famous people.
   (A) Cantankerous **(B)** Aloof **(C)** Apprehensive **(D)** Objective **(E)** Mercenary

3. We must base our scientific theory upon ____ fact, not upon your personal feelings about how the universe works.
   (A) Aloof **(B)** Apprehensive **(C)** Objective **(D)** Mercenary **(E)** Catastrophic

4. The ____ benefactor donated $10 million to the new library.
   (A) Apprehensive **(B)** Objective **(C)** Mercenary **(D)** Catastrophic
   (E) Magnanimous

5. Unless reversed, the continued melting of polar ice caps due to global warming may have ____ effects around the planet, causing water levels to rise and coastal areas to become flooded.
   (A) Objective **(B)** Mercenary **(C)** Catastrophic **(D)** Magnanimous
   (E) Cantankerous

6. Joe has no loyalty to his coworkers or the company he helped to build; his decision to quit and join the company's competitor for a slightly higher salary was incredibly ____.
   (A) Mercenary **(B)** Catastrophic **(C)** Magnanimous **(D)** Cantankerous
   (E) Aloof

7. The ____ man never smiled and irritably barked at anyone who came within his range.
   (A) Catastrophic **(B)** Magnanimous **(C)** Cantankerous **(D)** Aloof
   (E) Apprehensive

8. Surmount
   (A) Overcome **(B)** Undergo **(C)** Appease **(D)** Waver **(E)** Lecture or advise

9. Mollify
   (A) To create or manufacture **(B)** Waver or undulate
   (C) Reject contemptuously **(D)** Chastise or rebuke
   (E) To calm or soothe someone who is angry

10. Vacillate
    (A) Yield to another's authority **(B)** Boost or support **(C)** Overcome
    (D) Waver or sway indecisively **(E)** Flood or overwhelm

Paradox

an apparent contradiction; a statement that seems self-contradictory or absurd but may, in fact, express truth; a person or thing exhibiting a contradictory nature

Think of: **Parrot ox**

- Say aloud, "This sentence is a lie," and you have created a **paradox**.
- **Paradoxically**, the new process that was engineered to fix flaws in the system has only made the problems worse.

Acute

sharp, severe, intense, keenly perceptive

Think of: **A cute**

- The football player was carried off the field after he suffered an **acute** concussion.

- The problems of hunger and violence in East Africa have been made even more **acute** by drought and global warming.

Circuitous

roundabout, not direct

Think of: **Circle to us**

- Because several trees had fallen and blocked the main trail, we could not take a direct path to the lodge and had to follow a **circuitous** route around the mountain.

- The writer's path to literary acclaim was **circuitous**. He labored for years as an unsung tutor, self-published author, and even a gardener before receiving widespread recognition for his texts.

Remiss

negligent, careless, lax, slack

Think of: **Rent missed**

- Jan has been so distracted at work by her personal problems that she has been **remiss** in performing even the basic duties of her job.

- My electricity has been cut off because I was **remiss** in my payments and six months behind on my utility bill.

Prescient

having knowledge of things before they happen, prophetic

Think of: **Pre-see it**

- While the U.S. subprime mortgage and financial crisis of the late 2000s caught many by surprise, a few **prescient** analysts had been warning of potential problems for years.

- Some people may believe in Groundhog Day, but I'm skeptical that a rodent or its actions could prove **prescient** in predicting the weather.

Munificent

generous, **magnanimous**, **philanthropic**

Think of: **Money I've sent**

- Bill Gates, the billionaire founder of Microsoft, is also known for his philanthropic work and is considered **munificent** because of the large sums of money he gives to charity.
- The woman's **munificent** gift to the university has enabled the institution to expand its library and upgrade its facilities.

Malleable

capable of being shaped or formed, easily influenced or persuaded

Think of: **"Mallet-able"**

- For many people, the college years are a time when worldviews are formed, when **malleable** young minds latch onto the philosophies that will become the basis of their values for life.

- A blacksmith makes his or her living on the **malleable** property of metals. When heated, a metal can be easily shaped, or melted and poured into a mold, to form useful objects.

Expropriate

to take possession of, to take ownership of another's property

Think of: **Ex-property**

" IT WAS MY PROPERTY BUT NOW THAT THE BANK HAS
EXPROPRIATED IT, IT'S MY EX-PROPERTY. "

- The revolutionary government of that nation has such an anti-culture, pro-religion fervor that all the museums in the country have been **expropriated** and turned into houses of worship.

- While many intellectuals once embraced the idea of communism, most realized that it was unfair to **expropriate** one individual's land and possessions with the intention of redistributing them to others.

Usurp

seize and hold by force, use without right or authority

Think of: **You swipe**

- When the vice principal of that school tried to appoint a new teacher, the principal accused her of trying to **usurp** his decision-making authority.

- In 1825, the Russian military plotted to **usurp** power from Czar Nicolas I, a plot known as the Decembrist Revolt, but the coup d'état ultimately failed. (Note: *coup d'état* = the sudden overthrow of a government, usually by force.)

Prodigious

impressive in size or force, extraordinary in amount or extent

Think of: **Pro DJs**

- The boy made a **prodigious** leap from the tree branch in an effort to reach the lake with his jump and avoid landing on dry ground.

- American swimmer Michael Phelps's **prodigious** talent was evident in the 2004 Olympics when he won six gold medals. After his accomplishment, magazines ran funny articles about Phelps's prodigious appetite and the piles of pasta he consumed to fuel his workouts.

1. In the refugees' tent city, the lack of sanitary conditions and outbreaks of
    disease have made the crisis even more _____.
    (A) Acute **(B)** Circumspect **(C)** Remiss **(D)** Prescient **(E)** Munificent

2. Our gardener has become extremely ____ in his job, and as a result there
    are weeds growing throughout our yard.
    (A) Circumspect **(B)** Remiss **(C)** Prescient **(D)** Munificent **(E)** Malleable

3. A ____ president should be able to anticipate a military conflict and
    prepare for the event ahead of time.
    (A) Remiss **(B)** Prescient **(C)** Munificent **(D)** Malleable **(E)** Prodigious

4. Stu is fixed in his beliefs and closed to other people's ideas. I wish he would
    be more ____ and, at least sometimes, allow others' views to shape him.
    (A) Prescient **(B)** Munificent **(C)** Malleable **(D)** Prodigious **(E)** Acute

5. The money I've sent to all those charitable causes should prove that I am
    _____.
    (A) Munificent **(B)** Malleable **(C)** Prodigious **(D)** Acute **(E)** Circumspect

6. It is wise to take a _____ approach to starting a new business by carefully
    considering potential weaknesses in the business model before investing
    any money.
    (A) Malleable **(B)** Prodigious **(C)** Acute **(D)** Circumspect **(E)** Remiss

7. The flamingo's pink color is due to its _____ appetite for shrimp, which in
    turn consume large quantities of minute creatures with a high
    concentration of pink carotenoid pigments.
    (A) Prodigious **(B)** Acute **(C)** Circumspect **(D)** Remiss **(E)** Prescient

8. Paradox
    (A) Insight, keen judgment **(B)** Hatred, belligerence **(C)** Deceit, trickery
    (D) Partially completed document **(E)** An apparent contradiction

9. Expropriate
    (A) Evacuate **(B)** Inherit **(C)** Donate or give to charity
    (D) Overcome or surmount **(E)** Take possession of

10. Usurp
    (A) Improve or upgrade **(B)** Lift or elevate **(C)** Create a diversion
    (D) Seize and hold by force **(E)** Appease, placate, mollify

Evade

to escape or avoid, especially by cleverness or trickery

Think of: **Avoid**

" I'VE FIGURED OUT HOW TO <u>AVOID</u> HAVING TO PAY FOR THESE. I SIMPLY EVADE THE SECURITY GUARDS. "

- I advise against shoplifting because it is wrong and because there is little chance that you will **evade** all of a store's security mechanisms and avoid capture.

- When the victim's neighbor nervously **evaded** the detective's questions, the police began to suspect him.

Eminent

of high rank or quality; prominent, distinguished, renowned

Think of: **M & M's**

- The company created a $1 million prize to be awarded to one **eminent** scholar whose research improves lives in the developing world.

- In 2007, the **eminent** scientists Edward Wilson and Peter Raven predicted dire consequences for the planet's biodiversity if current trends in consumption and environmental degradation are not reversed.

Strenuous

demanding great physical effort or energy; taxing or requiring exertion

Think of: **Strength out of us**

- The **strenuous** climb up the mountain depleted the hikers' energy.
- After her surgery, Jen was told to stay in bed and avoid **strenuous** activity.

Unorthodox

unconventional, untraditional, breaking with custom or tradition

Think of: **Unearth docs**

THAT IS AN **UNORTHODOX** WAY TO STORE YOUR HIGH SCHOOL DOCUMENTS.

I ADMIT THIS IS A LITTLE **UNORTHODOX.**

THE **UNORTHODOX** STORAGE SYSTEM REQUIRES SONYA TO UNEARTH HER DOCS EVERY TIME SHE WANTS TO REVIEW THEM.

- To bury your old school papers in the backyard would be an **unorthodox** storage system and would require you to unearth the documents every time you want to view them.

- The basketball coach made the **unorthodox** decision to put his five smallest players on the court at the same time.

Partisan

1. noun – a fervent or militant supporter of a cause, a proponent of one party or faction 2. adj. – partial to or favoring a specific person or party

Think of: **Party son**

- During World War II, French **partisans** formed an underground resistance movement to fight the Germans, who had seized their country.

- The vote on the new bill in Congress was divided along **partisan** lines, with every Democrat supporting the measure and nearly all Republicans opposing it.

Baroque

1. extravagantly ornate; **florid**, complex, convoluted
2. pertaining to a style of architecture, art, and music prevalent in Europe in the 17th and 18th centuries and characterized by free use of ornamentation

Think of: **Bar oak**

THE INTRICATE ORNAMENTS ON THE BAR OF OAK MAKE ITS STYLE BAROQUE.

- Many visitors to Prague, capital of the Czech Republic, marvel at the beauty of the fairytale city, distinguished by magnificent **Baroque** architecture and centuries-old buildings.

- Joe dislikes that writer's **baroque** style and wishes the author could write at least a few simple, unadorned sentences.

Palatable

acceptable to the taste, agreeable to the mind or feelings; delicious, delectable, savory

Think of: **Pal at table**

PALATABLE FOOD IS YOUR PAL AT THE TABLE.

- Most Americans find Asian cuisine to be very **palatable**, which explains the profusion of Chinese, Indian, and Thai restaurants in the U.S.
- Few citizens of that country find the idea of raising taxes to be **palatable**, even though the government desperately needs the revenue.

Voracious

consuming great quantities of food, **ravenous**

Think of: **Vera ate shoes**

SHE WAS SO **VORACIOUS** THAT VERA ATE THE SHOES RIGHT OFF HER FEET.

- Tiger sharks, considered among the world's most **voracious** eaters, consume a wide range of prey, including crustaceans, fish, seals, birds, smaller sharks, squid, turtles, sea snakes, and dolphins.

- Julie comes across as intellectual and articulate because she is a **voracious** reader; she devours five books per month on a wide range of topics.

Progenitor

a direct ancestor, a person who originates or indicates a direction; a founder, **precursor**, or **predecessor**

Think of: **Produce generations**

MANY PEOPLE CONSIDER CHUCK BERRY, ELVIS PRESLEY, THE BEATLES, AND THE ROLLING STONES TO BE PROGENITORS OF ROCK 'N ROLL MUSIC, BECAUSE THEY PRODUCED GENERATIONS OF FOLLOWERS.

- Art critics and scholars consider painters van Gogh, Cézanne, Gauguin, Seurat, and Matisse to be among the most influential **progenitors** of Modern art.
- People who consider the Bible to be literal truth view Adam and Eve as the **progenitors** of all humanity.

Puerile

childish, immature, foolishly juvenile

Think of: **Pure child**

- It was strange and unsettling to hear my esteemed college professors engaged in such **puerile** conversation about their top ten farts.

- Marc thought he could impress Kim with the humor of his practical joke, but she was repulsed by his **puerile** behavior.

1. The army recruits had to undergo a very _____ regimen of workouts and drills all day long.

    (A) Eminent **(B)** Strenuous **(C)** Unorthodox **(D)** Baroque **(E)** Palatable

2. While my friend Tony likes that author's adorned, _____, and stylized form of writing, I prefer more straightforward prose.

    (A) Strenuous **(B)** Unorthodox **(C)** Baroque **(D)** Palatable **(E)** Voracious

3. Musical great Jimi Hendrix was considered _____ in his guitar playing; he broke new ground and revolutionized the use of amplifier feedback and stereophonic phasing.

    (A) Unorthodox **(B)** Baroque **(C)** Palatable **(D)** Voracious **(E)** Puerile

4. While many people are disgusted by the idea of eating fried grasshoppers or cockroaches, I find insects to be rather _____.

    (A) Baroque **(B)** Palatable **(C)** Voracious **(D)** Puerile **(E)** Eminent

5. The _____ doctor was well-known and widely respected for his humanitarian relief work.

    (A) Palatable **(B)** Voracious **(C)** Puerile **(D)** Eminent **(E)** Strenuous

6. The storm of locusts appeared suddenly and devastated crops; the _____ insects were able to devour the produce of entire farms within hours.

    (A) Voracious **(B)** Puerile **(C)** Eminent **(D)** Strenuous **(E)** Unorthodox

7. The teacher found the student's behavior to be immature and _____, especially when the boy began shooting spitballs in class.

    (A) Baroque **(B)** Unorthodox **(C)** Eminent **(D)** Strenuous **(E)** Puerile

8. Evade

    (A) Capture or seize **(B)** Invite or welcome **(C)** Neglect or ignore **(D)** Exacerbate, make worse **(E)** Escape or avoid

9. Partisan

    (A) Impartial decision **(B)** Founder of a dynasty **(C)** Inappropriate comment **(D)** A fervent supporter of a cause **(E)** An apparent contradiction

10. Progenitor

    (A) Prime example **(B)** Zealot or ardent supporter of a cause **(C)** A founder, precursor, or predecessor **(D)** Person motivated by money or financial gain **(E)** Person who gives to charity

Answer Key

Review #1
1a 2b 3e 4a 5e 6a 7b 8c 9d 10e

Review #2
1a 2c 3b 4d 5a 6a 7c 8e 9d 10e

Review #3
1b 2a 3d 4d 5a 6c 7b 8a 9e 10b

Review #4
1e 2a 3b 4b 5c 6d 7e 8b 9a 10c

Review #5
1d 2b 3a 4d 5c 6e 7a 8e 9b 10c

Review #6
1e 2b 3a 4d 5c 6a 7d 8b 9e 10c

Review #7
1b 2c 3a 4d 5c 6a 7e 8d 9a 10d

Review #8
1c 2e 3a 4b 5d 6e 7c 8a 9a 10e

Review #9
1b 2e 3a 4c 5d 6b 7a 8d 9c 10a

Review #10
1c 2b 3a 4c 5b 6a 7e 8e 9d 10a

Review #11
1e 2c 3a 4b 5a 6d 7d 8b 9e 10b

Review #12
1e 2d 3b 4a 5c 6e 7a 8d 9a 10d

Review #13

1a 2e 3b 4d 5d 6c 7a 8b 9c 10e

Review #14

1d 2a 3c 4e 5b 6c 7a 8b 9c 10e

Review #15

1e 2d 3a 4b 5e 6a 7e 8c 9c 10b

Review #16

1b 2d 3e 4a 5c 6b 7a 8e 9d 10c

Review #17

1b 2d 3b 4c 5a 6d 7e 8a 9a 10e

Review #18

1c 2b 3d 4a 5a 6e 7b 8d 9a 10c

Review #19

1e 2a 3b 4d 5c 6a 7c 8e 9b 10d

Review #20

1e 2c 3b 4c 5a 6d 7b 8e 9e 10c

Review #21

1b 2c 3b 4d 5e 6a 7e 8b 9c 10c

Review #22

1e 2c 3b 4a 5d 6b 7a 8c 9e 10d

Review #23

1d 2b 3c 4e 5c 6a 7c 8a 9e 10d

Review #24

1a 2b 3b 4c 5a 6d 7a 8e 9e 10d

Review #25

1b 2c 3a 4b 5d 6a 7e 8e 9d 10c

Index

Educators And Parents
Are Raving About VocabMonster...

the fun and effortless way to learn hundreds of new vocabulary words!

Here's what they say...

"VocabMonster is an absolute goldmine for those of us who teach vocabulary to middle-schoolers. Instead of force feeding students dull dictionary definitions, it's now possible to use visual mnemonics cues – an entertaining and rapid way to learn new words. I think it's absolutely great."

Fern Viola, Middle School Teacher, New York

"As a retired teacher, I have seen incredible results of visual association techniques for remembering information. VocabMonster is the best I've seen out there. I particularly love the many ways to learn – on the Web, on a tablet or iPhone, through books and e-books."

Lorraine Judelman, Retired Teacher, New York

"I'm a big fan of innovative ways to help kids learn and retain. VocabMonster fits the bill. It has a level of sophistication and flexibility that's above and beyond any competitor I've seen around. My verdict: it's a must-have for learning.

Jim Conley, Teacher, Chicago

"I wish VocabMonster was around when I studied for the SATs! Instead I was forced to learn all these vocabulary words by rote. Not so with my daughter. She actually loves the VocabMonster way of learning and I have noted a marked change in her strength of vocabulary."

Earl Van Horn, Teacher and Parent, Texas

"If I had to rate VocabMonster, I'd give it an A+. It makes learning new words so enjoyable and the meanings stick in my son's mind. It's revived his love of learning – and no higher compliment can be given to a learning resource."

Dana Wartell, Parent, Michigan

www.ingramcontent.com/pod-product-compliance
Lightning Source LLC
Chambersburg PA
CBHW060228050426
42448CB00009B/1352